W9-AJM-066

Grz

Good Stuff

Good Stuff

A REMINISCENCE OF MY FATHER,
CARY GRANT

Jennifer Grant

ALFRED A. KNOPF   NEW YORK 2011

This Is a Borzoi Book
Published by Alfred A. Knopf

Library of Congress Cataloging-in-Publication Data

Grant, Jennifer, 1966–
Good stuff : a reminiscence of my father, Cary Grant / by Jennifer Grant.
p. cm.
ISBN 978-0-307-26710-8
1. Grant, Cary, 1904–1986. 2. Motion picture actors and
actresses — United States — Biography. 3. Grant, Jennifer, 1966–
I. Title.
PN2287.G675G73 2011
791.43'028'092 — dc22
{B} 2011000454

Jacket photographs courtesy of the author
Jacket design by Carol Devine Carson

Manufactured in the United States of America
Published May 4, 2011
Reprinted One Time
Third Printing, June 2011

United as partners, my mother and father

brought a child into the world. Perhaps

a similar cocreative love leads me to write

this book. In honor of Mom and Dad's love,

and in gratitude for her wisdom, this

book is dedicated to my mother.

Contents

LIST OF ILLUSTRATIONS · *ix*

Chapter One · The Knee-Jerk "No" · *3*

Chapter Two · Archives: The Time Machine · *9*

Chapter Three · 9966: Freedom Has a Beautiful Structure · *24*

Chapter Four · Butter and Margarine · *31*

Chapter Five · Friendship Is Born of Respect · *40*

Chapter Six · Friends and Travel · *46*

Chapter Seven · Smart Women · *54*

Chapter Eight · Racetrack · *58*

Chapter Nine · Dodger Days · *61*

Chapter Ten · Acting · *65*

Chapter Eleven · Fame · 75

Chapter Twelve · Fame, the Lifestyle · 80

Chapter Thirteen · Society of Gossips—or,
Mind Your Own Business · 86

Chapter Fourteen · Mom & Dad—Mad at the Cookies · 93

Chapter Fifteen · The Beautiful English Woman
in Dad's Jennifer-Blue Cadillac · 104

Chapter Sixteen · Dad and Barbara · 107

Chapter Seventeen · The Grants · 119

Chapter Eighteen · It's Okay to Be a Pip · 124

Chapter Nineteen · Dad and Me: Slow Like Stew · 130

Chapter Twenty · Marbles Now or Horses Later? · 136

Chapter Twenty-One · The Phantom Pot Smoke · 139

Chapter Twenty-Two · Don't Marry the Guy
You Break the Bed With · 148

Chapter Twenty-Three · Polishing an Academy Award · 151

Chapter Twenty-Four · The Leach Potato Wart Cure · 153

Chapter Twenty-Five · My Father Was a Hottie · 159

Chapter Twenty-Six · Deeper Waters · 164

Chapter Twenty-Seven · Live with Death · 171

List of Illustrations

9966 Beverly Grove Drive, Beverly Hills, 1968 ii

Palm Springs desert, circa 1976 5

Vail, Colorado, circa 1976 8

Cary Grant and Jennifer, circa 1969 14

Jennifer Grant on the bus to school, 1970 15

Providence Saint Joseph Medical Center, Burbank, 1966 20

Envelope with flower from Jennifer to her father, 1969 21

Dad's illustration of an upside-down "wabbut" 22

On the front lawn of 9966 Beverly Grove Drive, Beverly Hills, 1969 23

Elsie Leach, Bristol, England, circa 1968 34

Elsie, Maggie, and Eric Leach, circa 1968 35

Jennifer Grant's fifth birthday candle, 1971 36

Palm Springs, circa 1972 39

Postcard from Dad, 1983 44

Jennifer and her mother, Malibu, circa 1975 44

Jennifer Grant's turtle drawing 48

The Hamptons, circa 1973 49

Palm Springs, 1970s 51

Madame Wu's Garden, circa 1971 56

57 *Audrey Hepburn's note to Grant, 1966*

57 *Aunt Marje, with Cary and Barbara, circa 1980*

62 *Grant's telegram to Walter O'Malley*

63 *Santa Monica, 1966*

64 *L.A. Dodgers ticket stub, Father's Day, 1969*

66 *Telegram from Prince Rainier, 1978*

70 *Grant's private plane, circa 1971*

71 *Telegram from Princess Grace, 1966*

72 *New York, 1969*

73 *Grant's handmade "Alphabet Book," circa 1972*

77 *Letter to Jennifer on her eleventh birthday, 1977*

82 *Letter from Grant, 1986*

83 *Grant and Jennifer, circa 1970*

90 *Willie Watson, circa 1973*

94 *Dyan Cannon, circa 1967*

99 *With President Gerald Ford, Century City, California, 1974 or 1975*

102 *Jennifer Grant, circa 1970*

102 *Note from Grant, circa 1978*

112 *Grant and Barbara Harris, 1981*

116 *Words of advice from Grant*

120 *Grant, Barbara, and Jennifer under the Golden Gate Bridge, circa 1980*

121 *Grant and Barbara's wedding day, 1981*

129 *Grant, Barbara, and Jennifer, 9966 Beverly Grove Drive, circa 1983*

134 *Cary Grant's letter to Jennifer, 1969*

141 *Hollywood Park racetrack, circa 1978*

144 *Grant's letter marking Jennifer's high school graduation, 1983*

149 *Telegram from Grant, 1972*

156 *Grant's birthday cake, January 18, 1982*

156 *Jennifer's first drawing, Beverly Hills, 620 Foothill Road, 1967*

157 *Letter from Grant, date unknown*

172 *Quotations for Jennifer, date unknown*

173 *Grant and Jennifer, on the steps leading to the lawn, 9966 Beverly Grove Drive*

174 *Note from Grant, 1973*

176 *Malibu's "shrimp show" horse show, circa 1978 or 1979*

Daddy attempts to put Jennifer to sleep. Jennifer wants to "read"
Newsweek *magazine as Daddy reads a book. Two-year-old Jennifer's*
words struggle to find their way out.

JG: Bend it.
CG: What, darling?
JG: Bend the book.
CG: One must always be careful with books and treasure them.
JG (blurts out): I love you. Will you hold my hand? (then) . . .
    Always be careful with books. Always be careful with
    books.

Good Stuff

Chapter One

The Knee-Jerk "No"

A few years ago, I visited a dear friend of mine, Yehuda Berg, for counsel. "You should write a book about your father." Right out of the clear blue sky. "No. I'm too private." "Well, all right then, write it for yourself, but you need to write." At home, for my eyes only, I wrote for an hour or so a day. Two days later, my friend Mark Teitelbaum called. "Hey, I just got back from New York. Met with a literary agent there about some stuff, have you ever considered?" "NO!" Damn it. Twice in a week. Once I could ignore. But two people, both recommending I write a book about Dad. That same week I was asked if I'd do a television special on Dad. Hmmm . . . Okay . . . here's my out. Maybe spending the next few years of my life delving and examining isn't necessary. I weighed the proposed television tribute. Alas, where Dad is concerned, it's all or nothing for me. The privacy policy won out. No to the show.

But for the first time, the possibility of a tribute lingered. The idea of writing . . . The moment my lips uttered no, my heart knew yes. Something about all that Dad gave me. I wrote every morning for a month.

IN MY FATHER'S LATER YEARS he asked several times that I remember him the way I knew him. He said that after his death, people would talk. They would say "things" about him and he wouldn't be there to defend himself. He beseechingly requested that I stick to what I knew to be true, because I truly knew him. I promised him I would. I've easily kept that oath. Although many books about him have been published, I've read none. Not out of a lack of interest. I'm sure there are some wonderful things I could learn about my father, but most likely more misconceptions than are worth weeding through. To me, he was like a marvelous painting. All the art historians wish to break down the motives, and the scheme, and so on. I would rather know, as I do, his essence. I believe that at the heart of a person lies passion. For the last twenty years of his life, I was given the extraordinary privilege to experience the full, vital passion of his heart. Dad used the expression "good stuff" to declare happiness or, as one of his friends put it, he said it when pleased with the nature of things. He said it a lot. He had a happy way of life. His life was "good stuff."

Just after my father's death, I graduated from Stanford. My senior year I had worked as an intern at an advocacy firm in San Francisco. My plan was to take a job with this same firm and later move on to law school. When Dad died I shifted gears in ten seconds flat. I felt pulled, in an almost subterranean way, home to Los Angeles. Why? If Dad came home, that's where he'd be. Have I been waiting for Dad to come home all these years?

At some level it's still hard for me to admit that my father died. I can talk about it and around it, but those two words. "He died." What can that possibly mean? That I won't get to hear his voice again? That's not true; I have movies, I have all his taped conversa-

A break from cantering across the Palm Springs desert. We likely stuffed ourselves with pancakes at Lindy Lou's before setting out. Circa 1976.

tions with me, I have pictures, I have slides. . . . I even have one of his sweaters in my closet. If I remember well enough, he will come back. He'll appear, out of thin air, at my door or in my living room, and we'll laugh and we'll hug and we'll talk and we'll hold hands, and maybe he can hold the baby while I make lunch for him. After all, he's a grandfather now. There's so much playing to be done. Watch out, baby Cary may pull your hair, Dad. And my dog, Oliver, is named after our mutual nickname, Ollie. In a Cockney accent we could greet each other with, "'ello Ollie! 'ow ya' doin', Ollie?" Oliver and baby Cary will look at us sideways, and then my father will never leave again.

To write this book is to fully admit, more than twenty years later, that he died. To move on with my life. The tribute to my father is more than mildly overdue. Dad has been deservedly honored by everyone and their mother. The U.S. government even turned my father into a stamp. For many years I've stayed silent. Other tributes to Dad stem from the perspective of show business, where the intimate side of his life is somehow vaguely analyzed, but never revealed. I am my father's only child. The world knows a two-dimensional Cary Grant. As charming a star and as remarkable a gentleman as he was, he was still a more thoughtful and loving father.

Madame Sylvia Wu, the marvelous restaurateur, was close to Dad for more than forty years. When I called Auntie Sylvia to discuss the book, she sweetly chided, "It's about time!" Sadly, several of Dad's closest pals, among them Frank Sinatra, Charlie Rich, and Gregory Peck, are no longer alive to share their memories of him.

Privacy was a gift our family worked hard to maintain. Selfishly, I have guarded my memories of Dad, clutching them to preserve that part of him that I alone knew.

Why didn't Dad write his own book? One archived audio cassette recorded in 1962 is a self-hypnosis session made for Dad. He was being instructed to exercise, gently, daily, and to write his autobiography. Presumably these are activities he wished to pursue, and he'd hired someone to help him with autosuggestion. The woman soothingly advised that he complete his autobiography with tremendous compassion for his subjects and not to worry, not to criticize the work, just to do it. Also, to exercise a bit each day. This was four years prior to my birth. Was Dad examining his life before having a child? Why didn't Dad finish his book? Did he consider revealing his history, his childhood, to the world? He never spoke of the endeavor, but he saved the tape for me. What turned him around? With so much misinformation out there, did he want to address and correct it? Is this why he stayed up at night? Was he too distressed about involving others' lives? Of course, his was the definitive voice. His parents were already gone. Any writing would have served Dad and Dad alone. Dad's parents weren't famous, he was. He knew his story. Anyone reading his story would have done so to learn about him. His motives were therefore the central theme. My guess is he came to terms with his past, and with anyone who wished to write about it. Let them examine their own motives. In my case, ultimately it's the same matter. Dad is gone; I write about him for me.

My hopeful guess on his attempted autobiography is that Dad was done with his homework. He came to terms with who he was and who his parents were. Let others play their guessing games. He trusted that those who knew him, knew him. Those who didn't, never really would. To make a case for himself would therefore be a fruitless, energy-wasting endeavor. He'd forgiven who he needed to forgive, let go of what he needed to, and accepted himself as he was. Archibald Alexander Leach, Cary Grant, and all.

It's important to understand the commodity of celebrity. In revealing my life, Dad's life, and including his friends, what is being "cashed in"? Privacy? Dad's name? There are certainly less all-consuming ways to make a profit. My conscience pulls, the way Dad's did. The only reason to write is to share the beauty of his life behind the curtain. I never knew Archibald Leach. I never really knew Cary Grant as the world thought of Cary Grant. I knew Dad.

Dad had two somewhat conflicting beliefs. He would remind me to never pay attention to what other people were thinking about me, because, he said, they were too busy thinking about themselves to really think about me. Funny. The polar opposite belief he espoused was "All you have is your reputation." The latter, I'm guessing, was learned through the business of "show" business. Dad has, and had, a deservedly glowing reputation. However, this belief in "reputation first" seems to have given rise to his fears of what might be rumored after his death. Then, there are interesting misconceptions about Dad. My choice is to leave these misconceptions to themselves. My hope is that we are wise enough with our own weak spots to allow great men theirs.

The grief of losing my father has come in waves over the years, as it does with most people. His love and devotion as a father provided my closest, most intimate relationship. Dad, and our time together, is in my bones. While reflecting on him, the memories themselves seem to boil down into certain "essences of Dad." My words, by their nature, are finite. Dad, now, is infinite. Still, perhaps these words can sniff around the essence of Dad's soul, to further elucidate the world's knowledge. Perhaps the old saying about the bird holds true: "If you love something set it free."

Many people long for a father's love. I had it. I have it still. Perhaps by writing this book I can transfer some of the love I feel for him. Perhaps Dad will inspire a daughter, son, mother, or father. If so, good stuff. I can hear my father's tone now, a little grumble with a Cheshire cat sparkle in the mix, "gooooood stuff."

Après ski on one of our rare trips to the snow. Dad didn't ski but filmed me making a mess of it. Here we're stuck on some Rubik's Cube–type game. Vail, Colorado, circa 1976.

Chapter Two
Archives: The Time Machine

A few years before I began this book, my stepmother, Barbara, alerted me that she was cleaning out "the vault." In the seventies remodel of 9966, Dad had an actual bank-quality room-size vault installed in the house. It took force to shut the six-inch-thick door and crank the steel handle down. Spinning the round numbered lock gave a grand flourish of control. Almost all of Dad's personal childhood archives were burned in World War I. Dad's goal: Nothing would rob me of my records the way the war robbed him of his. If the house burned to the ground, my childhood memories would be protected. In 2003, the shelves of boxes once held in the vault for me were transferred to my possession. Oh dear . . . my house isn't a vault . . . is everything safe? What's in all these boxes? What am I responsible for? My childhood home was no longer the place for my childhood archives. There were ten to fifteen large boxes. And boxes within the boxes. Each of them

labeled: JENNIFER'S NOTES TO DADDY, STANFORD, JEN-
NIFER'S DRAWINGS, ENGLISH TEA SET. All sorts of things,
all together, in boxes, on the living room floor of my Santa Monica
home. What to do? The tea set was and is gorgeous. Gold leaf. Tiny
roses atop the teapot and sugar bowl. One-sip cups fit for a proper
five-year-old's tea party. Other boxes were more confusing. Tapes.
What sort of tapes are these? Small quarter-inch somethings. Some
labeled with Dad's printing: JENNIFER AND ME, AT 9966,
MAY 30, 1971, SKIPPING AND LAUGHING. That's the title.
Skipping and Laughing. There's another larger tape, CARY'S
OSCAR. What sort of machine do I need to play these tapes? Are
they still good? Then there were cassettes. Maybe fifty. And Super 8
films. I opened every box, looked about, and then they sat in my
closet for almost a year, until I could wrap my head around the first
steps to tackling them.

The boxes contained photographs, slides, notes, cards, clippings, memorabilia, and Super 8 movies and audiotapes of me
growing up with Dad. The audio blurbs I've sprinkled throughout
the book come directly from these tapes. Until I was about twelve,
Dad took painstaking care to ensure that I had an accurate record of
my life. It is a firsthand account of the way he "saw" his daughter
through a lens and in his words. Dad entrusted me with a great
deal. The archives of life with my father are a precious piece of Cary
Grant.

The boxes are my own personal treasure chests. What amazes
me is the scope of his "Jennifer" files. He saved almost everything
he got his hands on. Dad wasn't a pack rat in other areas of his life.
Other than newspaper clippings, there were no stacks of stuff
around the house (even his clippings were filed and kept in a large
trunk). But when it came to me, anything I touched was fair game.
What should I do with the bar of soap on which I once glued a
squirrel's picture and multicolored glitter? Notes I'd crumpled and
thrown in the waste bin were taken out, hand ironed, stapled
together, and then dated and detailed in his signature red, capital-

ized type. For instance, SUNDAY, OCTOBER 29, 1978: WRIT-
TEN WHILE BARBARA AND I PLAYED CARDS is the caption
for notes I took, reporter style, of their card game of Spite and Malice. Dad saved a "recipe" I'd written for my lunch salad on April 27,
1979. It lists apples, raisins, longhorn cheddar cheese, Bac-Os Bits,
avocado, pastrami . . . I swear to you I can taste the salad now.

The articles he saved for me included the cautionary ("Wealthy
Women Fight Second-Class Treatment of Money Managers," "6%
of Psychiatrists Admit to Having Sex with Their Clients"); the
instructive ("Winning Ways for First Days on the Job," "Honda
Captures Its Second Consecutive Best Mileage Ranking," "Peace
Corps Picks Scores of Stanford Students," "To Entrepreneur, Success
Tastes Sweet"—an article on Mrs. Fields's cookie-selling success).
Other clippings are curio pieces: "Celebrity Dirt" (describes ven-
dors' travails in digging up literal dirt from celebrity gardens),
"Daddy's Little Girl Takes the Wheel and Daddy's in a Spin," "Pros
and Cons of a Delivery Room Audience," and the sardonic "Pity the
Rapist Who Can't Get Any Respect Behind Bars." Still other pieces
serve as a reminder of the decades that have elapsed: "Computer
Boom Hits Home for Stanford Students" features a photograph of
one of the original dinosaur boxes that foreran our now common
PCs. An Ann Landers column from 1972 (I was six) advises children on the handling of angry parents: "All that happens when you
argue back is that the adult argues back at you and on it goes, generally with the adult winning—and if not winning at least punish-
ing you for talking back, on top of everything else. Adults,
especially parents, don't like being called unfair—and they really
don't like it when they know they are! Which means that you will
have to hold back. You'll have to say the kind thing or be quiet.
And when you get a chance, do something loving which may help
the adult to get over what is making him angry." "The Little
Helpers Around the House" advises that "you're much more part of
the family when you all work together. . . . If your family is small,
if you are an only child, then you will want to be sure that your par-

ents understand your interest in wanting to help keep the home working."

Several of Dad's clippings give partial answers to questions I never before stopped to ask. Messages from the hereafter. For a long time I've vainly wondered if somehow I could've kept my father alive. Should I have found a way to save him? "Good-bye Dad, It's OK for You to Go" gave me a moment of solace. Perhaps he actually appreciated a lack of dramatic protestation surrounding his departure. One article describes a man predisposed to wanting a son who later revels, gratefully delighted by his fate as the father of four girls. "Is It Christian to Cremate" was likely meant to ease my mind with its assertion that "man is not a body, he merely wears one." One of my favorites, "Stanford, Where Rich Really Means Rich," tells of college life among the wealthiest from a scholarship student's point of view. This gives me unique insight into the way Dad viewed wealth. I was born with it. Dad worked his whole life to make and keep his money. "Who wants to look rich?" one self-important student asked the author. "Poor people." There was more than a touch of irony in the wealthy student's antimaterialism.

"In their eyes I was terribly materialistic, worrying about money, taking scrupulous care of my belongings so they'd last. But they could afford to be carefree spendthrifts, and untied to their possessions. They were, in fact, ready to renounce their worldly trappings and demonstrate the strength of their social consciences. You've got to have worldly trappings to renounce before you can renounce them. I hated to tell them, but poor people want material comfort and worldly trappings, and would never listen to these voluntarily penniless reformers denouncing the kind of life they were all after. . . . I worried about the next major expense and how to acquire some desired possession (typewriter, bicycle, etc.) while my friends worried whether to abandon theirs and find a guru. I worried about making a living, while they worried about meaning in their life. Which one is better off? Only a year ago I would never have thought to ask."

I didn't know "poor Dad" but here was his voice, and it explained the rubber band balls, coupons, and school-of-hard-knocks mentality perfectly. Dad gave me the resources—money, formal education, access, name—that he never had. But here's the rub: Having navigated an entirely different course in his life, how could he advise me to chart my course in this new sea of privilege? Dad couldn't take my courses, make my friends, establish me in business, and build on the platform with which he provided me. The most he could offer, the most any parent can offer, is the wisdom of sharing one's perspective, another vantage point. "You're so lucky to have what I never had" is often guilt-trip material. This article described exactly how I was lucky. It described my potential blind spots. The spots Dad tracked so that I never had to. When I returned home upon completion of my sophomore Political Science 1 class espousing the benefits of communism, Dad likely wanted to spit out his marmalade-covered muffin. Instead, he bought me *The Marx-Engels Reader* and suggested that after I devoured my new doctrine we discuss it. From recollection, the conversation went something like, "Yes, dear, lovely philosophy, but you see in practice, these people stand in very long lines for toilet paper . . . so it hasn't worked out so well."

Some things take on an entirely new significance now that I'm a mother. A simple note I'd written Dad, "Thank you for letting me spend the weekend at Lisa's." An entire weekend. Given his advanced age and the limited time we had together, letting go of a weekend was a monumental sacrifice. What made the forfeit worthwhile? My happiness, I suppose. I certainly wasn't aware of what that time really meant to him; I was simply shocked that he'd let me go for a weekend so I thanked him for it.

Safeguarding and modernizing the archives took time. The first job was to assess the materials. Photographs, slides, and letters I could cope with. Treat them gingerly. Find the right cases and covers to hold them. Easy enough. The cassettes were still in good shape, but too fragile to be played or overused. Who can be en-

*Dig the purse! Place
unknown, circa* 1969.

trusted with these? What's on them? They're mostly of Dad and me, I know . . . but these are every day at home or holiday or whatever they are tapes and my Dad's voice is all over them and what if they end up on some Web site? . . . Make lists. Next, I found some trustworthy souls to transfer the materials. Quarter-inch audio and cassettes became CDs. Super 8 films are now DVDs. With his meticulous print intact on the originals, I felt at liberty to watch and listen and get into our life together.

Dad presumably had a purpose in this vast undertaking of his. Home slides show an inordinate amount of orange furniture in our "original" prerenovation home. My current house sings with orange furniture and I've just ordered more. Then there are the jeans. In numerous childhood pictures I'm wearing jeans with two little button-down pockets in the front. I've worn the same style for

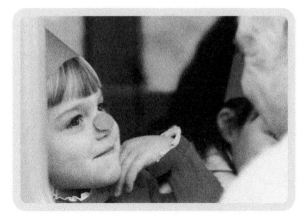

Taken during my daily kindergarten bus ride to school. Dad would wait alongside the road for a simple wave hello as we passed his parked car en route. This day the bus driver kindly stopped while Dad's secretary, Bill, snapped the photo, 1970.

the past ten years. My fascination is the link to behavior, the mind, personality.

How many thoughts, sentence structures, feeling states, do I wear, or surround myself with, that have their roots in a prerenovated life. When are my choices automatic? Programmed by my childhood comforts, ingrained likes and dislikes? Which decisions are conscious? How is it possible to discern the difference between patterning one's life, and simply repeating patterns? Dad had no records of his childhood. He did LSD to remember the past, to unburden himself with long accumulated "stuff." If I knew the past, perhaps I could reinvent what worked and toss aside what didn't. A circuitous route to presence . . . but sometimes the intellect is helpful that way. Until now I truly thought that I was the first in my family to like orange furniture. Guess again.

Perhaps Dad's longing for childhood recollections served as a guide. I had forgotten just how much he whistled around the house. How much he sang and danced. How patient and cheerful he was. Sometimes it's easier to forget all of those things. Did he know how much I'd miss him? Is that why he made all the tapes? It's as if he said, you want a day back . . . you want to spend time together . . . here it is! Live with me again. Hear the laughter, hear the silences, hear me walking down the hall, hear yourself bathing alongside your nanny, hear the TV, the phone, hear us preparing Christmas dinner. Here it is. Feast on it. You can have the days back. Pretty cool.

The fact that Dad saved everything for me speaks volumes about who he was. He didn't save just parts of it, the parts that might cast him in a favorable light, he saved it all. So many sweet notes from my mother. She sent glamorous letters from movie sets all over the world with intriguing return addresses including: Sloane Gate Mansions, London; Macedonian Palace Hotel, Greece; Tehran Hilton, Iran; and The Peninsula, Hong Kong. I know she was working, but it sounded great to me. Dad saved almost everything of mine that he got his hands on. He wasn't trying to write the story of my past by framing it through his selective lens. Some old friends of mine recently went through their scrapbooks and eliminated every picture of them with alcohol. "For the children," they said. "It's a bad example." So it's better to misrepresent yourself as pious teetotalers? Eliminate your past and play God with your children? What an impossibly confusing example to follow. That dictum speaks "Be who I paint myself as, not who I was" or "Do anything you want . . . only don't let anyone see it." My father left me smutty articles denouncing his parenting and chronicling supposed debacles between Mom and Dad, and columns lambasting him as an ex-husband and a man. One such article, written by a "close" friend of the family, cagily ended in praise. Thankfully, in reading the nonsense, my emotions ran second to my intellect. Some of it was true, but the angles! Baby with the bathwater behavior. What struck me was that someone who knew us well actually sold us out. What was he thinking? Was this my example of what not to write? How to steer clear of skewing my mind and my soul against family (thereby really revealing myself)? Yes, some of the facts were correct, but only a profit-seeking filtered adult mind could so grossly misinterpret them. Dad's audiotapes of me were labeled BUGS. What nefarious scheme do you suppose I was up to at the age of four or five? Dad wanted me to have it all. To freely go through, reminisce, and ultimately derive my own adult conclusions. He knew he could handle the ego-bashing, but could I? All he said in his defense was "I hope you'll know the truth." I do.

Some of my most treasured gifts are Dad's notes. His words have a way of inspiring me, still. Dad knew the joy of siphoning thought to word. He took time to craft his clever correspondences. Dad delighted in seeing the good in all things and finding ways to speak of it. In the age of e-mail, writing by hand seems a guilty pleasure. The paper itself is a gift. Thank God Dad saved all the notes. Hundreds of correspondences. Were I brought up in the nineties or thereafter we might not have all these letters on paper. We'd have . . . e-mails? There's something a bit sad about that part of progress. I have boxes of notes that show the progression of my handwriting styles and stationery. The curlicue phase, the block letter stage, the calligraphy. Do children e-mail their parents now? Dad would certainly print out the e-mails, but we'd miss a huge piece of their texture. I cherish Dad's handwriting! Its slant, force, and grace is personality in letters. Intonations in the texture of his print.

Oh, the clever, artful way he documented "stuff." At quarterly intervals, Dad mandated my relinquishment of clothing and toys for charitable donations. "You have so much, darling, give to those who need and will truly appreciate just one doll while you have ten." Jeez. What could I say to that? Dad would then photograph my giveaways by laying them about the 9966 house and garden. The ranch house, prior to reconstruction. If one stimulus didn't cue my recall, perhaps another would. My favorite T-shirt, with "HONEY" written in gooily dripping letters, sits on an old lawn chair. My tiny patent-leather shoes rest on the flagstone steps. I hear the screen porch door to my nanny Willie's room screech open. I've gone to get her and request her heavenly chocolate cake with powdered sugar in the frosting . . ."Pleeeeeeeeeease?" I just want to lick the spoon. "Maybe after school?" My first home, 9966 when it was a farmhouse. Next I'm in the old kitchen, pouring cereal out of a box, and there are weevils in it! Weevils in the Golden Grahams! My scream likely hastened construction by a year or so. Dad deduced this schematic memory-launching device on his own. And if the pictures of my things in my original home weren't enough, he'd taped years of events to make sure I had everyone's voices to fill in the blanks. Everyone's voices including my own. So odd to hear myself through the years. Sometimes I'm an impertinent brat— where in the world did Dad mine his patience from? Other days I'm a dulcet-toned angel child from heaven. And there's Dad's consistent, wind-chime-like whistling and singing around the house.

Friends have been somewhat awed by Dad's archives. I once shared an audiotape with a visiting friend. We listened to a small portion of a 1970s Christmas tape. Dad was documenting our opening of the gifts. So nice to hear Dad's happy laugh, and there I am at age nine, performing a newly learned magic trick for him. My friend smiled in amazement and then said, "That's your problem! That's why you haven't found a man. . . . How could anyone live up to that?" I tidied a sideways pencil. What to say? "You're right." No one can or will ever duplicate that sort of love. No one should. That was my father's place in my life. One needs only one father.

All of the photos, articles, notes, and things he kept for me were all lumped together. Pictures of me with President Ford next to my third-grade photo. My two-year-old doodles alongside a card reading "To Jennifer— With all the luck in this world and out— Neil Armstrong Apollo 11." The socially valuable commodities next to paper. It looked haphazard, though clearly Dad was nothing of the sort. Most of the stuff he saved was thoroughly mundane: "Good Morning Dad" scrawled on a Western Airlines notepad, "Sleep well" notes decorated with rainbows and horse heads, tiny "I love you" greetings . . . he saved boxes upon boxes of my notes to him. On the reverse side, in red capital letters, he typed the date, time, and where the notes were left for him. This is the stuff of love. These tiny moments are, ultimately, all.

How many times have I sat listening to a virtually blank hour-long tape? Voices in the background. Shuffling feet. A door slamming somewhere. "Hello's" voiced from someone or other we knew in those years. And then in the midst, Dad appears and says he's going to go sit by the pool and have his sandwich. I think he's talking to Aunt Mickey. Did Dad review the tapes before saving them? He was so damn organized, he must have. Perhaps Dad was a fan of the extended Pinter pause? If he reviewed the recordings then, the only answer is that he wanted me to have the time back. Normal days. Nothing much goes on. We sit around, play some games, have a bit of chat . . . This is it. Not every day is a graduation. The middle stuff of life. Value the middle stuff.

It's somewhat de rigueur for children to assess parents. (For example, she was a selfless mother or a heartless mother, or he was a beast of a father or a brilliant mentor.) But what of parents' assessment of children? What tips the scale in that department? My heart's ultimate question: Did I bring my father happiness? Much more happiness than sadness? Was and is he proud of me? Does every child wonder this deep down? Dad told me time and again how much he loved me, how proud of me he was. But he likely knew that my own judgment remained penultimate. When all's said and done . . . was I a good daughter? Well, the boxes of notes certainly cue my recall of the love I daily showered on him. As an adult, I must live with my own mistakes and forgive my personal shortcomings, but when it comes to remembering the way I loved you, thanks for giving me a leg up, Dad.

When will I stop missing him? Writing this book is challenging for me; however, going through the personal archives is . . . There he is . . . so clear. His voice. He's speaking to me again. Here come the tears. I feel so silly. Twenty-one years later and I'm still crying.

Our first day together. A moment of pure, perfect connection. Mom was exhausted after a grueling labor (Dad, who took the picture, threw his back out leaning over Mom). Providence Saint Joseph Medical Center, Burbank, 1966.

1969 · DADDY'S ROOM 9966 BEVERLY GROVE DR

It's time for Jennifer's nap but she's set on playing a game with countless chopsticks scattered atop the bed. Daddy gently coaxes with an impromptu song. . . .

CG: Because I love you, I love to take a nap nap. Because I love you, I love to take a nap nap.

Sounds of chopsticks click-clicking *together as they are shuffled about.*

JG: Which number do you want?
CG: Uh . . . [he gives in] number fifty-nine.

(Of course, the chopsticks aren't numbered, but with the flourish of make-believe, JG instantly hands him a chopstick.)

CG: Well . . . you found it so quickly.
JG: Which number do you want?
CG: Sixteen and three-eighths.
JG: Here's sixteen and three-eighths.
CG [laughs]: Thank you.

Jennifer fights sleep with her new game. Daddy can't help but enjoy himself. This goes on for some time, then . . .

CG: You count very well for a girl who's only three years and a little less than two months old.
JG: Let's make the airplane . . .
CG: You count very well and you also ride the bicycle and oh— what else . . . you also won't take your nap.
JG: Daddy, which number do you want?
CG: No thank you.
JG: Well then, do you want a lemon?
CG: What, darling? Where's a lemon?

Jennifer pretends a chopstick is a lemon.

CG [into tape recorder]: This is seldom effective, but I pretend to take a nap in the hopes that Jennifer will follow. It's, uh, not probable . . .

Dad pretends to snore.

JG: Open your eyes. Open your eyes, Daddy! No, don't sleep.
CG: Oh, I mustn't sleep? But it's sleep time, isn't it? It must be . . . it's three thirty and we haven't had our sleep. . . . Just think of that.

Dad did LSD, I do archives.

THE FIRST FLOWER – A Pansy – that Jennifer Ever Presented me. "For You, Daddy". From the Terrace of my house at 9986 Beverly Grove Drive, Los Angeles, California.
march 14th, 1969.

Marjorie Everett was one of Dad's closest pals. She ran Hollywood Park. Aunt Marje sent me a big bag of her own keepsakes.

My early nickname for Dad was Daddy Wabbut.
This upside-down wabbut is a perfect illustration of his
simple, silly sense of humor. The funny would be lost
in the translation — either you get it or you don't.

Articles clipped from newspapers along with business and personal correspondence. Dad loved his position as a director on Marje's board, and he took it seriously enough to take her to task if necessary. Their friendship could stand the mild friction.

My Dear Marje,

It occurred to me and possibly other outside Directors, that the monthly series of Hollywood Park board meetings are no longer truly necessary. With R.E.I.T. [Real Estate Investment Trust] firmly established, the Epicurean debt greatly reduced and soon to be eliminated, the problems attendant upon the building of new barns no longer of consequence, and with Hollywood Park running profitably and smoothly (thanks to the continuing efforts of you and Verne together with the executive staff and Neil), there is really no need for a meeting each and every month. Perhaps alternate months meetings of the entire board would suffice; unless, of course an emergency arises. Otherwise regular, or whenever convenient, meetings of efficient executive staff should be sufficient to continue running the track to the shareholders' and everyone's satisfaction.

Howard Koch is also writing a letter to this effect so I trust you and Verne will give our thoughts your kind and serious consideration.

With warmest regards, Cary

Oh . . . there's an article from the *University of Chicago Chronicle* about his death. He's dead. Oh no. The Nile erupts. What? Didn't

Afternoon cavorting on the front lawn of 9966, 1969.

I know he was dead when I was reviewing other bits and pieces just a moment ago? Did his letter suddenly bring him to life and now he's gone again? Well, in a way yes. Reading his letters, seeing his pictures, I'm brought back. I feel him. Then, seconds later, there's the objectification of a life before my eyes. Cary Grant, leading man, screen legend . . . dead.

My father is irreplaceable. To me, and I think, the world. He left a hole. Almost daily I see his films listed in the TV section. Whatever special blend of temporal and eternal grace he had still resonates. It reminds me of the way he left himself undefended to his critics. He had enough character to recognize that being great doesn't require perfection. The world hungers for that vibration. However, in growth, I stumble toward the graceful realization that it's illusory to cling to "Cary Grant" or Dad as the embodiment of an ideal. As with the best of the best meals, when you're full, you're full. As delicious as the food or drink may be, more isn't better. Stopping is the only way to enjoy the experience without compromise. Remembering is fine. Living is the apex.

Chapter Three

9966: Freedom Has a Beautiful Structure

9966 Beverly Grove Drive. Dad and I lived, slept, played, wept, dined, danced, and laughed there. We were always free to be ourselves at home, whatever that meant. Through the thick and thin of divorce, earthquakes, remodeling, and construction, we were at home. There's a beautiful symmetry to the number 9966, as if it were the end and the beginning of a quotation. The first time I remember seeing my father, and the last time I actually did see him, was at 9966. One of my father's priorities was providing me with a sense of permanence and stability. The actual structure he chose was a farm-style house. Our home atop a hill. The following quote is from a book my father kept at his bedside, Thoreau's *On Man and Nature*.

Every leaf and twig was this morning covered with a sparkling ice armor; even the grasses in the exposed fields were hung with innumerable diamond pendants, which jingled merrily when brushed by the foot of the traveler. It was literally the wreck of jewels and the crash of gems. . . . Such is beauty ever—neither here nor there, now nor then—neither in Rome nor in Athens, but wherever there is a soul to admire. If I seek her elsewhere because I do not find her at home, my search will prove a fruitless one.

Home was beautiful because freedom was at the heart of it. Throughout the years, in a few of his different Super 8 films, Dad recorded my outdoor play at 9966. At age two, in a sweet frilly dress and patent leathers, Dad films me as I run around the flagstone deck whirling-dervish style. Crazy circles, arms outstretched, to and fro, until I pounce on the lawn and roll down the grass hill. There goes the dress! Perfectly out of my mind. Some years later, Dad, his girlfriend Maureen, and I concoct our own seventies summer square dance on those same flagstone pavers. Dad, then seventy-one, was by far the best dancer. His long limbs, precise gestures, and natural grace pull focus immediately. Super 8 shows my girlfriend Lisa Lennon and me, at age eleven, as we perform human "horse shows" on the lawn. We devise an obstacle course and canter around it, changing leads as horses do and jumping over every stool or lawn chair in our path. Dad loved my playtime because I was clearly happy at home. He must have known that if I was free and happy there, I had a springboard for the world.

We lived in style, with many luxuries, but luxury is only luxurious if it doesn't tax the senses by being pointless. Dad liked things that worked. Practical stuff. A friend of mine recently introduced me to the term *"wabi-sabi."* While referring to my garden, and some roses that refuse to be replaced, he said that they added a touch of *wabi-sabi,* the Japanese art of seeing beauty in imperfection and profundity in nature. It's the way Dad lived. It's clean, it's graceful, it reveres all stages of life, and it appreciates inevitable decay. It's a way of being happily present and content with what is. It seems to be in line with Thoreau's thinking. Dad "got" that. He appreciated nature's wisdom. In nature, form and function are beautifully unified. Nature isn't wasteful.

Our home at 9966 Beverly Grove Drive was easy on the eyes because it was organized, but there was always room for the little bit of mess that accompanies life. The house was one story, which Dad always preferred. He liked to feel that everything was connected and easily accessible. In the actual front of the house (the side facing an extraordinarily expansive view of Los Angeles away from the street), was a flagstone deck and, beneath the deck, the lawn and pool. Our pool was occasionally a point of contention, at least as far as heating it goes. Dad experimented with the heating conundrum. Right around the time the heater went on, in fall or winter, I would stop swimming. It was getting cold; I didn't much want to be jumping into the water. Without the heater, the water temperature was frigid. Of course, after a few weeks, I'd get a yen for a swim and request heat. "Use the pool and then I'll start heating it. It's too damned expensive to heat if no one's going to use it." Heating the pool was wasteful. Even in California, the pool wasn't a big draw in winter. The heating bill wasn't worth the two or three swims I *might* take. The frigid water won. I remember occasions when I flew into its chilly embrace. . . . Wait for summer! So the pool was refreshingly cool all summer and brave cold in winter. If I really wanted to swim, I could drive down the street to my friend Jonathon's house and frolic in his *heated* pool! On the whole, Dad wasn't much into structured exercise, but he occasionally did laps during the warmer months, which, in California, is 90 percent of the year.

Dad introduced me to the sun on our front deck. "It's healthy to get just a bit of sun. Not too much." Funny. Now many people run from the sun, or at least shield themselves in its presence. Of course, the world is a different place now. The sun's negative effects weren't as widely known then, and "global warming" wasn't in the everyday vernacular. Still, we knew the sun caused premature aging, but Dad reminded me occasionally, "You're getting a bit pale, need some sun." Dad "took" about half an hour of sun every few days when we were at home. He always had a healthy glow. His actions spoke: "Enjoy this. Enjoy nature, let the sun kiss your face. . . . Yes, you'll have wrinkles. . . . Enjoy those, too." What is the choice, really? Our house was bordered on the west by a thriving avocado tree, an apple tree, and a lemon tree. There was a large island of calla lilies just outside the door. I loved the look of the calla lilies: smooth, open, and strong. The east side dropped into a ravine of eucalyptus. With nature surrounding our home and our bodies, it could more easily affect our thoughts.

Dad used to say that the state of your surroundings reflected the state of your mind. Also, there could be an inverse correlation. A clean atmosphere provides space for thought. This has become a truism for me. During college exams, regardless of my lack of sleep, my boyfriend used to marvel at the way I had to clean my apartment *before* studying. A direct offshoot of 9966. At home with Dad, everything had to be organized. Inside and out. Take his closets, for example. Everything was placed in order of color and length. Colors proceeded from light to dark. Shirts, pants, jackets, suits, and sweaters. Lined up or stacked, light to dark. Contrary to what one might think, he didn't have an immense wardrobe. His policies about waste ran across the board. He had clothes for every occasion, just not too many of them. And no . . . not *everything* at home was neat and tidy.

OCTOBER 20, 1969 · FLAGSTONE TERRACE AT 9966

Jennifer and Daddy cavort. Classical piano plays in the background. Daddy and Jennifer sing "Jack and Jill." Jennifer riffs on, improvising . . .

JG: Little Miss Muffett sat on his puffitt . . . and they followed Mary into the teapot.

CG: I don't know that song. . . . They followed Mary into the teapot . . . hmm.

JG [singing]: Mary had a little lamb . . .

CG: With some green beans and jelly . . .

JG: Daddy!

CG: Oh . . . sorry. Would you give us a concert again under the umbrella if we have some coffee cake and juice and coffee and milk?

JG: Mmm-hmm.

CG: Do you like that music, dear?

JG: Yes, I do!

CG: It's a Chopin waltz. And the man who's playing it is an old friend of Daddy's. His name is Arturo Rubinstein. [Then] How old are you now, Jennifer?

JG: (proudly) Three!

Dad credited music with transporting him beyond his habitual mind-set. Classical music generally set the tone at home. Days were infused with Beethoven, Bach, and Debussy. At day's end, with saturated minds, he added the lyrical joys of Frank Sinatra, Tony Bennett, or any manner of Sammy Cahn's stylings to soothe and entertain us. Dad was close with both Sinatra and Cahn. Lyrical magicians. In an offbeat mode, Dad would marvel at Uncle David's music. Mom's brother, David Friesen, plays the upright bass. Dad sat listening, fascinated, as Uncle David's jazz shot out of our stereo, my father's eyes wide with delight: "Your uncle is out there. . . . He's out so far I can't catch up." It's akin to hearing Robin Williams riff at comedy. Sometimes he takes a turn that just loses me in the dust. I wait, mind altered, eagerly anticipating his return, as a catcher might wait for a fly at home plate. For musical playtime, Dad "doodled" self-taught tunes on the piano. Some of his own concoctions, other songs he practiced by ear. He was a damn good doodler, really.

Dad tried for years to interest me in piano, and for a while, I was startlingly average at it. Dad was present for my one note pecked at a time, bungled recital of "We Three Kings" when I was eight. Later, a miserly, abusive piano teacher scared me away entirely. Whenever I'd miss a key, she hit my finger with her fist. Never forgot it. I didn't "tell," undoubtedly due to some misplaced respect for authority, so sadly, despite Dad's urgings, I never returned to my lessons.

My typical teenage jam-out music boggled Dad's mind. As noted, Dad enjoyed either wordless, classical music or lyrics with meaning, timing, and style. So my heavy "pop" phases were like nails on a chalkboard at home. Occasionally he granted me radio station privileges on the way to school, and invariably ended up calling the music rubbish. "Any moron could write that. Baby baby, love ya love ya, need ya need ya. Hogwash." If we were at home and the decibels forced him from his perch down the hall, he would lean in the doorway, cross his arms, and with his best con-sternated look growl, "Oooooh, what a pip you are." I liked it. I sort of enjoyed the mild chastising. Made me feel spunky. Most of the time I was, by natural inclination to his ideas, obedient. Yes, I liked Sinatra, Chopin, Beethoven, Stravinsky, Cole Porter, Tony Bennett, and Sammy Cahn. Just throw in a little Foreigner and Led Zeppelin and it's all good. Dad and I had a sixty-year generation gap between us. Much of what Jennifer Diane Grant found "cool" Archibald Alexander Leach deemed preposterous. If I was going to play the Top 10, at least I could keep the volume below 5.

Our most profound and habitual music was silence. Silence meant independent thought. Silence meant we were digesting ideas, learning new ones, or simply meandering in essential down-time. Perhaps because I was an only child and there were fewer feet at home, or more likely because it was an established ritual, silence was a comfortable atmosphere at 9966. We knew we were all there . . . doing our own "things" . . . Dad might be reading in his club chair, Barbara taking a bath, while I did homework, made a snack, or otherwise entertained myself . . . but there was always the requisite space for midday silence. No one knocking at the door. No one affirming themselves with peekaboos or hellos. Everyone left to their own devices. Solitude in numbers. Active silence. At once asserting our individual parameters and defining a familial respect. There is something deeply comforting in knowing that your family is happy enough to leave you alone, knowing you'll bring the new-found treasures of solitude back to the table soon enough. It's a great preparation for the world. An unwritten pause. Whatever our own meditations were, we left one another the room to muse.

1967 · TAPE RECORDER IN MY CRIB

CG: Good morning, brown eyes. Say something Jennifer. Talk to them.

(no response)

CG: There are certain similarities we have. Eyes, hands . . . Jennifer, come try to walk. Come to me. Try to walk.

Jennifer crawls over to investigate Daddy's bookshelves.

CG: They're beautiful, aren't they? Beautiful books. Oh yes, I do, I have beautiful books that you'll enjoy and treasure and cherish. Yes you will because you like books, don't you? Now we look at books—all the beautiful things. Pictures, you see. Careful. Be very careful. These are very fine books.

Chapter Four

Butter and Margarine

Dad and Jennifer play as assistant David cooks pork chops for dinner.

CG: Can I have a pork chop with fat on it please, sir?

Later same evening . . . Jennifer's bathroom

Jennifer being bathed by Willie. Daddy whistles in the background.

JG: Oh, this soap smells marvelous. I'm four years old. I'll be five.

CG: You mustn't rush your life. You must enjoy every moment —so take your time until you're five. [Then] She's rubbing herself down with a towel. She has the sweetest little figure you've ever seen and she's just been to England to see her grandmama.

Our family loved to eat. On weekdays, dinner signaled the end of work. Postdinner, nothing needed to be accomplished. There wasn't a single evening Dad worked after supper. Dining meant time, effortlessness, and freedom from "doing." Whether Dodger Dogs or the extravagant elegance of Chasen's restaurant, we savored our experience. Meals lasted an hour or so; nevertheless, Dad admonished himself for rushing.

"Everything in moderation, darling. . . . If you eat less, you'll live longer. My mother ate like a bird and lived to ninety-two." Though he occasionally grumbled, Dad managed to abide by his principled moderation. Still, he was no renunciant. Dad spent his life surrounded by fine food and drink, and he enjoyed it. While Dad was known for his refined nature, his palate was an exception. Sure, Dad enjoyed good, quality food, and even haute cuisine, but really he just loved to eat. He used to swear that he couldn't tell the difference between butter and margarine. The Hollywood Park directors' lounge buffet was a perfect example. The food was fine, but it was no Chasen's. Still, how the platters taunted him. They were logistically challenging, as well. We had to pass the buffet each time we journeyed to place a bet. Damned éclairs! The racetrack was minimally a four- or five-course day. So when we went to the track for the afternoon, we skipped the evening meal as penance. Dad generally drank white wine with dinner, and on occasion he drank a Gibson. Dad's "Gibson" was vodka and dry vermouth with a pearl onion. He was funny about his wine. After a glass he'd make an off-color remark about something, and follow it with, "Oh! Watch out for me, I'm drunk!" Then it was time for what I call his happy foot dance. He'd wiggle his feet back and forth and, with a childlike grin eclipsing his features, say, "These are my exercises, you know, I'm an old man now." (He was, astoundingly, never an old man. His mind kept him young.)

Sometimes after dinner I'd make a play for Dad's candy drawer. Yes. He had an actual drawer filled with candy. Well, I guess it wasn't really full, but it always seemed so. Although there were other cakes, cookies, and things in the pantry, this was the place for his most cherished sweets. The candy drawer contained a good deal of chocolate, some marzipan, lemon drops, and lots of hard candies. Dad said hard candies were good for your throat, so I scored on those when I had a cold. He especially liked Cadbury chocolate. When he visited England, or the Tudor shop, he'd bring me my favorite, Cadbury Flake bars. Flake bars are quite literally thousands of chocolate flakes stuck together, which ingeniously melt in your mouth the moment they're consumed. Dad had a hard time letting go of his "sweeties," even when they began to turn. I usually found a few overly hard marzipan fruits or some whitening chocolate in there. If I didn't like it, I could "keep your mitts out of my stash." Dad grew up during the war, when waste was preposterous, so we forgave him his hardened marzipan bits and he forgave us our trespass. He would often tell of the stockpot he grew up with, "You just didn't waste food . . . throw it all in the pot, a bit of a carrot, a potato, on a rare day turkey . . . and it was damn good."

Lots of our family rites revolved around food. Mom and I had a fetish for lychee and reddy black cherries. The produce stand at the corner of Pacific Coast Highway and Topanga Canyon carried our favorites. We gorged ourselves on bags full of the summer delicacies. Dad and I ate more fatty foods together. For some reason most of our favorite "joints" were in Santa Monica. He loved the fish and chips at H. Salt. The fish was flaky cod. I can still smell the vinegar. We bought our fresh fish at Santa Monica Seafood. "Darling, are you ready for this smelly place? All right then . . . Let's get some halibut, just for the halibut!" Goofball. The Tudor House, then on Wilshire Boulevard, was another hot spot. Walking into the Tudor House was a departure from the Los Angeles world as we knew it. Where else could you sit surrounded by dainty floral wallpaper in priory chairs eating gooseberry tarts with afternoon tea and take home bangers and mash to boot? We got cases of frozen bangers (the fatty English sausage) at holiday time. Barbara made them a part of our annual Christmas party. Very British of us. It must have

Lovely, ladylike Elsie Leach. I wish I remembered more stories Dad may have shared of his mother. She is still, in large part, a mystery to me. Picture taken by Dad, Bristol, England, circa 1968.

reminded Dad of his hometown, Bristol. At Christmastime we had multiple traditions. There are definite advantages to being from a split family. Many holiday dinners are the norm.

FEBRUARY 12, 1969 · BRISTOL, ENGLAND· ELSIE'S NURSING HOME.

(Grandma Elsie was a petite, pert, five-foot-something, ninety-five-pound woman with an owl-like gaze and devilish grin.) Dad's cousin, Eric, Eric's wife Maggie, and Elsie celebrate Elsie's ninety-second birthday in fine fish-and-chip style.

Maggie: Would you like just a spot of wine, Elsie? Or some brandy? Brandy warms the cockles of your heart.

CG: Here's to your ninety-second birthday. God bless, happy thoughts. Nothing like a fish-and-chip birthday. It's the best type.

Lots of eating and small talk about the Snooty Fox restaurant. Later, Grandma Elsie speaks into tape recorder.

Elsie: Arch . . .

CG: I love you very much, you know that, don't you, Mother?

Elsie: Yes, and I love you, darling.

Smiling for Dad's rare presence in Bristol: Grandma Elsie Leach alongside Dad's cousin Eric Leach and wife Maggie Leach, circa 1968.

A sweetly odd tradition came to be our 9966 Thanksgiving dinner. One of my favorite foods on the planet was Peking duck. Auntie Sylvia introduced me to it at Madame Wu's Garden. Well, one Thanksgiving, to assuage my yearnings, Barbara asked what I might like with the turkey meal, along the lines of "nuts or berries with the stuffing?" My pip daringly replied, "Peking duck, please." Lucky for all of us, Barbara can cook. It went off so beautifully that from then on, Barbara prepared the traditional Chinese dish as our Thanksgiving supper. The process was quite elaborate. Barbara navigated Chinatown to fetch two whole ducks, which then hung, death-penalty style, in our kitchen to dry. By the third year Dad placed a bow tie on the neck of the "male" duck. If they were going to hang in our kitchen, they might as well dress up the place.

Recently Barbara and I traveled to an Indian spa in the Himalayas. "Ananda" translates as bliss . . . and it was. In L.A. life I'm a devout yogini, so everyone presupposed that India meant incessant yoga and meditation. Nope. We spent most of our time eating. We exercised a bit, but mostly, we simply relaxed together. It was family time off. True to form we found several hours a day

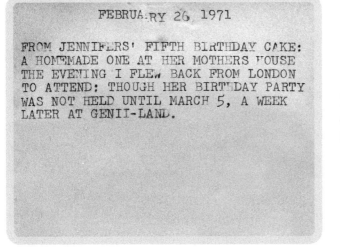

FEBRUARY 26, 1971

FROM JENNIFERS' FIFTH BIRTHDAY CAKE:
A HOMEMADE ONE AT HER MOTHERS HOUSE
THE EVENING I FLEW BACK FROM LONDON
TO ATTEND: THOUGH HER BIRTHDAY PARTY
WAS NOT HELD UNTIL MARCH 5, A WEEK
LATER AT GENII-LAND.

*The candle is still
contained inside
this envelope.*

where our schedules diverged: "Meet you at lunch" or "Meet you at the Vedanta lecture." Perhaps we both needed a reminder of the 9966 days. Awaken midmorning and eat a little. Sun a little; swim a little; eat a little; read a little; walk a little; eat a little. Ananda.

Our 9966 docket labeled weekdays as work, communication, and activity time. Nighttime was all about easy entertainment. Couch-potato style. Lots of TV. Weekends were for backgammon, cards, and puzzles. We spent countless hours playing games on the huge, dark, leather club chairs in Dad's room. How anyone managed to properly sit in those damned slippery cushioned chairs is beyond me. At game time I held my cards with one hand and my balance with the other. Somehow, easily upright Dad religiously sat in his club chair for the daily ritual of coffee (black), *Los Angeles Times,* and *Wall Street Journal.* Cover to cover. Our card game of choice was Spite and Malice. It requires two decks and sometimes half a day to complete.

At night, we'd have our dinner together, on trays, in the bedroom, in front of the television. It was totally normal and exquisitely comfortable. I've thought about the traditional paradigm of the family sitting down for supper. That's the time when everyone breaks bread together, discusses the day's events, bickers, laughs, and bonds. Not us. Because Dad was retired, we had all day for those activities. "Retired" is actually an ill-fitting word for my father. Not a day went by where he wasn't active in business. He was on the board of many companies, and, like a venture capitalist, fascinated by the puzzle of each. Following busy, rarely dull days, nighttime was for relaxation. With trays perched in front of us, Dad and Barbara on the bed, and me at a bedside table, we dined. Before Barbara lived with us, I was on the bed alongside Dad. I must admit that I felt thoroughly debunked at the side table—I mean, I grew up there! After twelve years as the resident female, who was this British woman who was taking my place at dinner? I spent my crib years in that room! My crib was in the front of the room, closest to the window, separated from Dad's bed by a stereo, about ten or fifteen feet away from him. Somewhere around the age of two the crib was traded in for a sweet, child-size bed. It had a miniature pull-out desk on the side where I could do my coloring. Very fancy. I still remember being in the crib. I remember seeing his big face, head, and hands resting alongside me. He used to reach over the edge and adjust my toys and things. He would talk to me in a smooth, low voice and sometimes sing to me in that same voice. He had a record of his songs that he played now and then, as he sat, or mostly stood, by my crib. At night, when he slept, I could hear him snore. He did it with gusto. Mostly, I slept right through it. He always felt close. At some point I was moved into my own room, but at dinner I was queen bee next to Dad again. So . . . what right did Barbara have to take my spot on the bed, when I'd had dibs since I'd been in a crib? After dinner I'd hop up there with them for a bit before bedtime. Barbara and I would trade shoulder rubs while we all watched TV. Dad relished that time. I imagine it made him feel we had become a complete family. New territory for the Grants. So shoulder rubs following dinner was our new tradition. Suited me just fine. It was our cozy, day-is-done, dumb-down, chill-out time. What better than TV to accompany?

So there we are at dinner, all perched in front of the telly. The Grants were fans of sketch comedy, game shows, and documentaries. Standard weekly fare included *The Carol Burnett Show, All in the Family,* and Dad's favorite, *60 Minutes,* a Grant Sunday ritual. Dad cherished Andy Rooney's segment. Andy Rooney had a way of making the mundane hysterical. The newsman's Seinfeld. *The Carol Burnett Show* scored big points when an actor broke face. Mischievous fun masquerading as work was just Dad's cup of tea. Onscreen and off my father oozed "I'm having the time of my life. . . . Catch me if you can." Dad took the world and all its affairs seriously lightly. Tim Conway's old man (the one who mimed geriatric-paced flashing with his trench coat) brought down the house. Like Mr. Magoo, the old man narrowly escaped disaster, pissed off anyone without the patience of a saint, and astounded everyone in his path. Dad and I used to imitate him around the house. With crossed eyes, donning invisible trench coats, we'd fake flash each other at a snail's pace. The accompanying sound is "Waaaaaaaaaaaaaaaaaaaaaaah." Dad also loved Benny Hill. He busted up at that slight, old, bald man patting all the pretty things' heads. Wish fulfillment, perhaps? When I managed to control the clicker, Jacques Cousteau won out. Nature documentaries were also standard fare. Wild animals of the Kalahari, whales of the Pacific, or whatever little varmints we found interesting. My personal TV quota was generous, even on school days. Dad occasionally looked askance at my less than intellectual fare of *Bewitched, I Love Lucy,* and *The Brady Bunch.* But I was responsible with homework, received consistently good grades, and always kept a tidy room, so . . . if TV was my guilty pleasure of choice, he let it go. *All in the Family* was the only sitcom we watched together. Dad loved Carrol O'Connor's Archie.

Archibald Alexander Leach. I don't think my grandmother, Elsie Leach, ever fully accepted Cary as Dad's name. Who can blame her? She named him Archie. God knows, if my friends so much as uttered a slight derivation of my name, they were hastily corrected. Wonderfully embarrassing. Here's the scene: The telephone at 9966 rings, Dad answers. "Hey, is Jen there?" Dad gives a guttural throat clear and says, "I named her Jennifer for a reason." In a lesser mood he might simply scold the caller with "Her name is Jennifer, not Jen." A bit of bite. So, true to the family stripes, until her dying day my grandmother referred to Dad as Archie. Carrol O'Connor's Archie was continuously beleaguered by his family's antics. He was always going off at Edith's imbecilic comments or Meathead's leftist ramblings. While daughter Gloria pulled her own ridiculous gaffes, she was by and large spared Archie's wrath. Me too. Dad had one, rarely used nickname for me: Modigliani. Dad thought I had a nice neck. It's nowhere near half as long, tapered, and elegant as any of Modigliani's sirens . . . but I still dig the nickname. Every once in a while he'd cast a gentle glance my way, murmuring, "There's my Modigliani."

How is it possible to look the way he did at seventy-two?
Palm Springs, California, circa 1972.

Chapter Five

Friendship Is Born of Respect

My father consistently spoke in glowing terms of his loved ones. Barbara, his mate and companion, was "That Barbara! Isn't she amazing. The most organized, thoughtful, talented woman . . . and she's a delightful cook." Dad would literally sing at the thought of her. Dad marveled over his pal Kirk Kerkorian: "Brilliant man! Kirk doesn't flaunt his wealth. He's quiet and reserved. He studies things carefully." In describing me, he'd say, "You're a happy soul" and "You'll have a happy life." To me, that's one of the kindest things he could have said. He was right. Reminding me of this fact may have cemented it. Perhaps Dad recognized it in me, or perhaps he knew that times would get rough and he wanted me to know my own strength. I'm not sure which came first, but, no matter the difficulty, whatever tribulations I may have faced, I've always felt happiness at my core. If it's true, why not fill your child with this belief? Knowing my father thought this has given me strength.

Although my father was naturally kind and charming with people, he restricted his inner world to very few. My mom's mom, Clara Friesen, often reminded me, "If you've got three friends, it's a lot." Who has time for more? Intimacy takes time. From my perspective, Dad's closest companion was Stanley Fox, his personal manager of many years. I remember the long conversations Dad held with Stanley. The wise laughter. Dad and Stanley learned from each other and respected each other's opinions on politics, money, and family. Stanley was reserved, with a penetrating, slow gaze. He made thinking look attractive. When Stanley did speak he was forthright, direct, and gently self-assured. We sometimes visited with Stanley and his wife, Jewel, at their home in Brentwood. Jewel served delicious coffee cake. Over the years, Dad and Stanley acquired similar characteristics. Vocally and physically they came to mirror each other. After Dad died, I visited the Foxes. I was immediately struck by Stanley's gestures. It was as if a piece of Dad were sitting in front of me. His modulated voice, thoughtful listening, and economic gestures were Dad's. They even dressed similarly. Gray slacks, button-down shirts, and cashmere sweaters.

Dad's friendships endured. Every year we had a small Christmas dinner, and every year the same friends showed up. Quincy Jones and Frank and Barbara Sinatra were regulars. Sometimes Gregory and Veronique Peck, Johnny and Alex Carson, Kirk Kerkorian, Merv Griffin, and Eva Gabor joined us as well. Once or twice David Hockney joined us, as did Sidney and Joanna Poitier. Kirk was by far the most private of the lot. Unless we were on family vacations, most of the time Dad and Kirk visited by themselves. They were buddies. Kirk said that there was never a moment of dissension, of any sort, in their twenty-five years of friendship. They were introduced by the owner of the Las Vegas Dunes Hotel, Dad's buddy Charlie "Kewpie" Rich. In Kirk's words, from the moment they met, Dad was consistently humble, kind, and terrifically smart. Takes one to know one. They held a profound respect for each other's accomplishments, which, though different, were similar in scope and magnitude. Both were mavericks in their respective fields. "Kirk's a self-made guy. His parents were Armenian immigrants. He started from the ground up. Flew a single-engine prop plane and built his business into all this."

Dad's friends were highly successful people from all walks. While achievement distinguished their ranks, kindness was the common denominator. Likes attract. It's common to hear that success necessitates cutthroat behavior. What an unfortunate belief. Focus, yes. Diligence, yes. Decisiveness, check. My father shared a birthday with Muhammad Ali. Though I never saw them together, it was lovely overhearing their annual, joyous "happy birthday!" phone calls. In actuality, Muhammad Ali's birthday is January 17 and my father's is January 18, but they carried on as if it were the same day. Muhammad Ali's autobiography places a conscious emphasis on kindness. His race brought him face-to-face with outrageous bigotry, but he turned righteous anger into fuel for change. The ultimate kindness. For Dad, much of the time love meant simple kindness.

One of Dad's deepest dislikes was witnessing thoughtless behavior. He couldn't tolerate it in himself or others. When Dad said, "Oh, how unkind," it reflected his sadness at a person's lack of consideration. It was an indictment of character. The war baby side of my father knew the value of little in times of need. He made rubber-band balls and clipped coupons. So if I carelessly threw out half of a delicious peach, I might hear "Oh, how unkind" as he lifted the sweet treat from the wastebasket to inspect my folly. It truly saddened him. I often wonder what my father would think of the world today. Particularly the state of the environment. My bet is that Dad would be big into recycling and drive a Prius. He'd scowl at my gas-guzzling car and trot off in his conscious choice.

Dad's friends have been good to me. When I was about ten

years old, Dad took me to hear Frank Sinatra at the Hollywood Bowl. Front row center. I felt pretty in my white cardigan sweater and patent-leather shoes. Somewhere early in the concert, mid-lyric, Frank stopped singing. There he stood, directly above me onstage. "Jennifer, I love you, Jennifer." Oh dear. Wow. Heart stopped. Dad got teary. Me? Really? Lucky me. Big moment. I wasn't embarrassed, just awed. Still feel it. Perhaps it warmed Frank's heart to see Dad and me together. Barbara Sinatra said that often women would swear that Frank was singing directly to them. The little girl in me wanted to protest, "But he really did! And I loved it!" Many years later, in an entirely different format, Frank stepped up for me again. It was nine years after Dad's death, at our annual Christmas party; I was twenty-nine and freshly divorced. It was all I could do to dress for the party and people could see it from a mile. There's a certain condescension that's masked as concern. The "Oh, I'm so sorry . . ." Stepford thing. Well, I was up to my ears with it and leaking blood all over. Frank and Barbara were seated near the fire in the study when I hobbled over and cuddled up next to Frank on the couch. I can't remember who approached me next with the customary "Oh, dear Jennifer, I'm just so sorry, what a tremendously difficult thing. . . ." Frank cut him or her off at the pass. "She's just fine, thanks. Anything else? . . . How you doin'?" Instant blood transfusion. It was a tiny moment, but he knew me. He knew just how to deflect and protect.

Dad and Frank were gifted with the indefinable incandescence of charm. They were high on life and they radiated. Their containers were well honed, structured, and self-defined. They surrounded themselves with stringent supporters. Their give-and-take required a high level of circuitry and tolerated few leaks. So where others might gush that high feeling, they let it out in a constant stream. They flirted with almost everyone and everything and life graciously flirted right back.

Dad liked romance and made friends with couples who knew how to dance its dance. Hollywood royalty. A March 2007 *Vanity*

ROYAL VIKING STAR - ROYAL VIKING SKY - ROYAL VIKING SEA
World Class ships of Norwegian registry. And spirit. World
Class - it's a level of elegance, comfort and spaciousness.
What's a class above First Class.

Length: 581 feet - Tonnage: 22,000 GRT
Crew: 300 - Passengers: Approximately 500.

AT SEA.

MPO GUAM, GU
FEB 4

96921

POSTAGE DUE 93¢

PRINTED IN SWITZERLAND

WE'RE HERE TODAY AND
GUAM TO-MORROW, WHILE
WISHING YOU WERE GUAM
TO BE WITH US — BECAUSE
WE'LL BE GUAM QUITE A
WHILE; BUT YOU'RE ALWAYS
IN OUR THOUGHTS, dear
JENNIFER. Much much love
Barbara and Dad.

JENNIFER DU GRANT.
SANTA CATALINA SCHOOL.
MARK THOMAS DRIVE,
MONTEREY, CA 93944
U.S.A.

*LEFT: I love Dad's penman-
ship, and his tiny drawing of
the ship is almost architectural.*

*BELOW: Mom and I headed
for our 98 Malibu Colony
home. The puffball of fur
behind us is our poodle au
natural, Lovie. Circa 1975.*

Fair article compared "Old Hollywood" with "New Hollywood." The "Old Hollywood Power Couples" roster included Walter and Carol Matthau, Ronald and Nancy Reagan, Lew and Edie Wasserman, and Billy and Audrey Wilder. Weird to think of them as "power couples." Power what? Ronnie and Nancy? Billy and Audrey? Billy was always such an instigator and Audrey with her long cigarette holder . . . they're a power couple? Hold on . . . I'm all grown up now . . . this should make sense . . . but it's puzzling. Couple objectification. In my mind, "power couple" connotes Bill Gates and Paul Allen. The *Vanity Fair* article objectified lot of married couples were Dad's buds. All of them. Yeah, I knew them too, in that "I better sit up straight and they're always nicely dressed and pretty cool to me" adolescent sort of way. However, even adolescent Jennifer knew that above and beyond that, clearly these spouses loved uniquely. They were joined at the hip. In my experience, these people shared uncommon bonds. Maybe *Vanity Fair*'s got something here. Maybe that kind of love translates into power. Too romantic a thought? You should've seen these couples.

Chapter Six

Friends and Travel

Dad and his friends traveled together, and traveled well. Cruising was one of the favorite "family" vacations. From the start Dad enjoyed trips at sea. "Terrific concept. You unpack once, visit several places, and always maintain your traveling home. Good stuff." Plus Dad could loosen the reins on me a bit. Wherever I was, it couldn't be too far off. He and Barbara read or played backgammon on one of the various decks while I swam, played shuffleboard, or otherwise skulked about the ship with various new pals. Kirk and his children cruised Alaska with us. It was such a hit that Dad's pal Charlie Rich (Uncle Charlie) joined us the following year, and then Auntie Sylvia a few years down the line. We traversed Sitka, Juneau, Ketchikan, and Glacier Bay. This was back in the day when major glaciers abounded. Dad was his usual shutterbug self, but magically Kirk isn't in any of the pictures. Literally, not one. We ate together, went to shows together . . . communed. How does one entirely avoid being photographed on a two-week cruise? Kirk was always on the quiet side. Shy? Not really. The type that sits back and takes it all in with his eyes. Kirk says only what needs to be said. Zero small talk. That meshed just fine with Dad.

Our vacations were generally to the same spots. Not necessarily because they were his favorites but because he was comfortable in them. Comfortable meant being with friends. Surroundings, although notably beautiful, were secondary. Privacy was important, quiet was essential, and happy companionship was key.

WESTHAMPTON — PALM TREE MAGIC

1972 · ZEILER HOME · WESTHAMPTON, NEW YORK

Dad, Aunt Mickey, Jennifer, and others enjoy a barbecue picnic lunch on the front lawn. Dad Polaroids the goings-on.

CG: When I was little she looked exactly like me . . . and our eyes . . .

Aunt Mickey: Jennifer has your elegance and charm. Very unique. But physically she looks like her mom.

CG: No. When I was a child I looked exactly like that.

Norman and Mickey Zeiler's place was an annual home away from home in the seventies. Norman was a New York buddy who ran Bill Blass clothing. Uncle Norman hooked Dad up with wholesale shopping. As Barbara Sinatra recalled, "You know, your father had interesting friends. He had friends from all walks of life. I remember I was shopping on Seventh Avenue in New York one time and I came out of one of the big buildings and there's a big black van with black windows and everything and I hear someone say, 'Barbara, Barbara.' And they slid the door open and it's your father. He's shopping too." Uncle Norman taught Dad the fashion

June 19th 1971.
At WESTHAMPTON L.I.. N.Y

My turtles apparently had extra legs.

manufacturing business. This trickled down to no designer jeans for Jennifer. "Are you kidding me? They make those blue jeans in the very same Hong Kong factory as say . . . Gap jeans. They all cost about twelve cents to put together and then mark 'em up all down the line until the ridiculous designer comes along and slaps on a whopping five hundred percent to put their name on you. Forget it! Forty dollars for jeans is unheard of. We'll go to the Gap and get you the good as the rest of them twenty-dollar jeans. You'll look a hell of a lot smarter, too." Dad and Uncle Norman drank martinis, talked political economics, and shared heartwarming laughs. Most important, Uncle Norman and Aunt Mickey had a pool, so I could splash about from dawn to dusk.

During one of our many summer stays in the Hamptons, I was seized with intense pangs of longing for my turtles. I simply had to find them a gift. New plastic palm trees were in order immediately. Well . . . Westhampton wasn't exactly booming at the time. After warning me of probable disappointment, Dad obliged and we took *The Jenny,* my namesake outboard motorboat, into town. Dad's Walter Eckland names a similar boat *Jenny* for a silent little British girl in the film *Father Goose.* Uncle Norman saw the movie and found the coincidence charming enough to follow suit. As Dad docked *Jenny,* I bolted down the short pier toward the alley. The only stores at the local dock were a gas station and hardware store, and the alley running between the two. Waiting for Dad to tie up *Jenny,* I spied a little brown bag alongside the alley. As I ran ahead and merrily snatched it up, he called, 'Darling don't touch that—it could

I can still feel the perfect ease of our Hamptons summer days, swimming, boating, tennis, reading, and backgammon by the pool with burgers. Divine. Circa 1973.

be—" Too late. My newly opened bag contained a set of perfect plastic palm trees. "Daddy, look! For my turtles!" His knees practically buckled. No, Dad hadn't somehow stealthily planted the gift. He stopped dead in his tracks, agog and wide-eyed with a true double take. "Well, I'll be damned. It's magic." My first lesson in synchronicity. Dad told the story for years.

Our number-one weekend getaway was to Uncle Charlie's Palm Springs estate. Uncle Charlie was a staple in our life. Kewpie was maybe five feet tall, bald as they come, with a year-round tan (sometimes orange out of the Coppertone bottle — which Dad heckled him for) and a heart that never stopped giving. Dad and Kirk met through Kewpie in the early seventies. Uncle Charlie lived in a Spanish adobe on several acres of manicured, palm-tree-lined property. I learned to drive a golf cart and play putt-putt on that lawn. We stayed in the pool house, near the good-for-guppy-hunting pond and gorgeous rose gardens. And there, just a few miles away, we discovered Smoke Tree.

From age six on I rode with Dad at Smoke Tree Stables. Smoke Tree was a unique rental barn in that they set you free. You could mount up with a group of pals and canter over an expanse of desert without a guide. Freedom and togetherness. Dad believed in horseback riding. Dad and Quincy had a unique spin on the usefulness of the sport. One of Quincy's young daughters loved horses. "It's great," he said, "it keeps her away from guys." Dad shared a similar, he thought Freudian, philosophy. "Girls are into horses until they discover boys. . . . It's all about having something between the legs." *Dad!* Is that why you taught me to ride? Forestall my interest in the opposite sex? Nice try. Dad put me on a horse when I was eight months old. Nothing like planning. Mom and my nurse, Beulah, stood alongside as I rode a pony on the beach in England. When I reached the ripe age of one, Dad placed me atop a thirty-three-year-old chestnut gelding. Relatively little chance for a mishap there. Start slow, start slow.

Palm Springs was all play. Even the two-hour drive time to and fro. In those days there were no handheld computer games, video-monitored seats, or cell phones. Imagination was necessary. So Dad stocked the Cadillac with word scrambles and hangman, and we concocted distance games. I chose a landmark ahead — a street sign,

The guesthouse and seldom vacant pool at Uncle Charlie's Palm Springs home, 1970s.

a bridge, a 76 station, and so on, and closed my eyes until the guesstimated goal. Mundane, yes, but at least it kept me occupied. Once there, Uncle Charlie's was a desert Disneyland. We rode horses in the morning, swam, played poolside games, and putt-putt golfed all day long. Dad held the backgammon title. Occasionally I pulled off a win, but only through sheer luck of the die. Dad knew the odds of particular rolls, and the quick, stock moves. A six-one roll closes out the spot next to your home board, and so on. Dinner was time for word games. "In my basket" was a favorite. Each person places an imaginary item "in my basket." Concentration. Miss the order of objects, you're eliminated. Another favorite, "Loves coffee and hates tea," went something like this . . . I know a woman who loves pound cake and fries, but can't bear the thought of peanut butter. And it's all because she loves coffee and hates tea. Loves the peach but hates the tree. Loves cars but can't stand automobiles. For "Loves coffee" we needed a fresh guest each time. Once you're onto the secret, it's cake. We played silly games constantly. How the adults tolerated it, I'm not sure, but Uncle Charlie's place was my adolescent wonderland.

MONACO . . . PALATIAL ABANDON

Dad loved Monaco. What's not to love? Owing to his close friendship with Prince Rainier and Princess Grace, we stayed at the palace. We dined in the private quarters, with Rainier, Grace, and some combination of Caroline, Albert, and Stephanie, depending on who had what plan which night. We ate loup de mer, cocktailed on the terrace overlooking the Med, rode in limousines over the cobblestone streets, and somewhat let our guards down together.

The level of palatial luxury was off the charts. During one visit, while we were greeted after arriving from the airport, having a cup of tea with the royal family, our bags were sent to our rooms and unpacked. This led to a good gaffe. In those years, Norma Kamali's shoulder pads were all the rage. My soft black tie-around-the-waist jacket had shoulder pads virtually up to my ears. Hip. The shoulder pads were removable, so they could be placed in other flat shouldered garments as well. Well . . . my jacket was hanging in the closet, but no pads. The next day I discovered my bikini had never looked so good.

We visited Monaco's annual circus festival three or four times. The best acts from around the world converged. Trapeze artists, dancing bears, clown acts, aerial artists, Russian dancers, tigers, elephants, the whole nine yards. Dad was one of the judges, so we sat front row center, in the same box with Rainier and Grace. At this time I'm nine, ten, eleven, and the circus is a favorite outing. Dad is seventy-two, seventy-three, seventy-four, and he's equally awed by it all. His adolescent septuagenarian face lit up watching men fly through the air. He would gasp with relief as grasping hands snatched the aerialists to safety. He'd show me the grip: "It's wrist to wrist, darling, hands can slip." Hmm, I'd think . . . remember that for future something or other. He photographed damn near every act. It was fun to sit next to Dad at the circus. He'd smile till he cried. Did it remind him of his youth with the Pender Troupe? He spoke of it occasionally: "Darling, the floor was all wood, and to open the show I would run out . . . I had to practice this many times when the stage was fully lit, because come performance time the lights were out and I had to find a specific point in the floor to dive in. . . . You see there was an invisible trapdoor in the floorboards, so out I run with "Let the show begin," and *boom!* I dive straight through the wooden floor! I gave the audience quite a gasp." He liked to brag about his limber stilt-walking as well.

After the circus we'd go back to the palace "disco room," where everyone unleashed and unwound from the night's festivities. The disco room was a tiny little pub-ish feeling bar downstairs with a jukebox so the kids could play music and dance around. Sometimes Princess Stephanie and I wandered off to play Operation in her room. The game's object is to gently maneuver tweezers to remove bones from a magnetic patient.

Funny, I still remember my concern about leaving school for those trips. I'd be gone a good week and a half or so and we arranged that I could take my lessons with me. But what new songs might I miss on 93 KHJ? What if my friends were on an entirely new page and I missed a crucial moment? Zeppelin might fall from favor and I wouldn't know it.

Chapter Seven

Smart Women

Dad worked with most of the most spectacular women of his day. He was accustomed to sharing ideas and banter with the ladies, on-screen and off. While he didn't maintain day-to-day friendships with his costars, he did find a few amazing women to pal around with. Dad appreciated women with business acumen. One of his nearest and dearest friends was Madame Sylvia Wu. Sylvia created Madame Wu's Garden, our most frequented restaurant. Dad met Sylvia just after she stuck her toe in the water with a small place in Santa Monica. Dad was smitten. Madame Wu credited Dad with initiating her ascent in the landscape of L.A. cuisine. Word of Dad's patronage spread and Madame Wu's received media attention. Soon, Madame Wu had a following. All the stars, politicians, and muckety-mucks ate at Madame Wu's

Garden. Her restaurant was elegant, comfortable, and gave the illusion of privacy. Booths had space between them. You'd never bump elbows with the group next door. It provided the rare experience of being out and maintaining boundaries. Madame Wu lures you in with her sophisticated, gentle demeanor and then polishes you off with her savory cuisine. Happily, Sylvia is now auntie to me. This woman has business in her bones. At a recent lunch I asked Auntie Sylvia where she garnered her savvy. She gave a sweet shrug—"I don't know." Dad must've smelled it in her. At ninety-four, she's as elegant as ever. For the past thirty and then some years I'd swear she's flawless. She wears her jet-black hair scooped into a large bun and consistently dons her signature Chinese silks, pearls, and large-frame glasses. Her eyes dance with curiosity and, while conservative to the core, her minxlike bearing intimates serious fun. How she gets away with her candor, I'll never know. She's craftier than a Southern belle. Auntie Sylvia once informed my charming, handsome beau and me that we weren't suited for marriage and all the while made it sound like a compliment. Perhaps it was. Auntie Sylvia is a total knockout.

Where Auntie Sylvia is all about charm, Aunt Marje the stalwart is all about the unpolished facts. In-your-face style. Aunt Marje came from a racing family. She eventually held controlling interest in Hollywood Park racetrack and managed almost every inch of it herself. CEO overtime. Delegation was heretical. Aunt Marje was and is one tough cookie. I know because after college she put me to work at the track. She started me with an entry level job in the Operations Department. Carrying my father's crocodile briefcase was perhaps over the top. No one so much as dotted an "i" without her permission. Racing is Aunt Marje's lifeblood, from the liniment to the racing forms.

At age eleven, with my father's permission, Aunt Marje arranged for me to learn "real" riding. Aunt Marje hooked us up with Charlie Wittingham, a world-class Thoroughbred trainer,

who in turn found me a tireless coach. Mary McGlemere exercised
racehorses for a living. This female Rocky rolled straight out of bed
to her one-hundred-push-up breakfast. Mary knew and loved
horses and had the patience for teaching me to sit a trot, pick a
hoof, and ride bareback . . . all of which Dad filmed. *And* I learned
it on the backstretch of the track. Super cool. There were pros
everywhere. Thoroughbred handlers, exercisers, grooms, and trainers. I can still smell the alfalfa. The environment was intoxicating.
I was like a wobbly ankled kid with new ice skates. Let 'em all
stare . . . it was a blast.

LA PAISIBLE
TOLOCHENAZ
VAUD — *Suisse.*

Dearest dearest
Dyane and Cary
We are all so
ecstatic and happy
happy. happy. for
you Both — had
no idea where to
cable as do But
hope this reaches

you to give you
my heartful of
blessings love
and tenderness —
for your marriage
for your baby
for _you_ .

♡
× × × × × ×
Audrey

Sadly, I never met Audrey Hepburn. Befittingly, she wrote her congratulations note with a fountain pen, 1966. Their magnificent chemistry on-screen seemed to be quite sweet offscreen as well.

Aunt Marje didn't smile for everyone, but she always smiled for Dad (with Barbara).

Chapter Eight

Racetrack

Aunt Marje was Dad's entrée into the business of horserac-
ing. Dad was enchanted. The racing world reminded him
of the studios. Dad studied the workings of the track with
the same diligence he'd applied to his career. He knew the bones of
the place and delighted at giving new guests a tour. It resounded
like a good family story that gets passed down through generations,
but with fresh energy in each delivery. He spoke of Hollywood Park
as one might delight in a child who'd just been accepted to an Ivy
League college. The monologue went something like this: "The
track has a subculture all its own. Right up front are the parking
lots and their tremendous staff. And the guys are pretty person-
able . . . you'll see. Once inside the main gate you find your tip
sheet guys hootin' their picks for the day. I never follow 'em. Jennifer's a pretty good handicapper. . . . You could follow her just as
well." (Cheshire cat grin from me.) "Inside the pay gate is the main

pavilion, the 'dirt' track, and the turf course, with the infield at center. All of which require upkeep and care. The infield is akin to a golf course in terms of watering needs. Inside the main pavilion is a virtual restaurant row." Now, here's where Dad really lost it. The food court was no restaurant row. It was more of a mini mall doughnut spree environment. Grease galore. But something about it fascinated him. I liken it to the adolescent "new pack of bubble gum" feeling. A whole pack. Imagine all the individually wrapped pieces. All the chewing excitement and the bubbles. I walked a bit taller with a new pack of gum in my pocket. That was Dad at the food court. He turned giddy. The food court was the main attraction of the tour. Sometimes he'd save it for in between the third and fourth race. "In a little while, we'll go down and I'll show you the food court!" Sigh. "Look at that, there's a Mexican joint, a barbecue place, ice cream shop, salad bar . . . anything you like! And all of those places have to be stocked, managed, and operated. Think of the staff for that alone." Now, we sat in the Directors' Lounge, two stories up . . . the chichi of racing . . . but Dad dragged all his guests down to see the damn food court. "Up above us takes you to the PR Department and track announcers. You know, it's a deceptively large place, there are maybe sixty thousand people here today. Let's check the tote board for attendance. Isn't it amazing? Computers tally the ever-changing odds on each horse and the infield display board keeps a running tab of favorites and long shots for each race. There are several levels of viewing, each of which has their own group of betting cages and ticketers. There's the grandstand, the boxes, the Turf Club, and the Directors' Lounge. Now, what you don't see, behind the scenes, is the back track. The back track is home to stable boys, exercisers, veterinarians, racehorses, stable ponies, dogs, cats, you name it. The guys are back cheering for their horses. . . . Take a look through the binoculars. Along with them come the natural provisions of food, shelter, and medical supplies. Quite an enterprise. Isn't it just the damnedest thing? . . . Shall we go get an éclair?" Livitup, Dad.

The Directors' Lounge was a home away from home. Fellow Hollywood Park directors Walter Matthau and Mervyn LeRoy, Dad's dear friends, sat nearby. Sometimes Mervyn drove with us when his wife, Kitty, wasn't accompanying him. Stanley Donen and Quincy Jones sometimes joined Dad and Barbara as well. Funnily enough, Dad gambled very little. Five or ten bucks a race. I think I once saw him bet fifty. Maybe. He was too busy cooing. I inherited the nongambler gene. While doing a series in Vegas, over the better part of a year I never placed a single bet. Flying into LAX offers a tremendous gander at Hollywood Park. Dad loved to point it out from the sky: "Look at the size of that place. . . . It's a city within the city." Hollywood Park was on the short list of oft-visited venues.

I suppose we rarely ventured out because it created such a spectacle to do so. Once a particular outing such as Hollywood Park became established, somehow the crowd parted a bit easier. People still noticed Dad, but they generally didn't trip over themselves with astounded awe. Maybe that's why stars create such amazing homesteads. Perhaps there's more to it than big bucks and showing off. Home needs to be a haven. It's *the* safe space. If you can't go to the park and sit peacefully with your children, better have a damn good lawn! People laugh at the absurdity of stars having bowling alleys instead of basements. Actually, I do too. But if you had any idea what an absolute pain in the ass it is to go anywhere with someone the entire world wants to be close with . . . it somehow starts to form an absurd logic. Movie theater at home! A gym with a private trainer! Bring people in who don't glaze over at the sight of "CARY GRANT!!!!" I'm pressing the point. We had none of these things at our house, but I understand how one gets there. We managed to forge our semisecure venues, if only a few.

Chapter Nine

Dodger Days

The 1970s Dodgers were our team and Dodger Stadium was a regular outing. Steve Garvey, Ron Cey, Steve Yeager, Davey Lopes, Manny Mota . . . those Dodgers. Dad was friends with the benevolent O'Malleys, so Dad and I sat in the owners' box with dear Walter, Kay, and their son Peter O'Malley. From age four or so, I learned the RBIs and ERAs of baseball from Dad and the Dodger family. Dad eventually bought loge-level season tickets. "It's on the same level as the owners' box, darling." There were perks to the freedom of everyman seating. For one, I was allowed to go purchase our Dodger Dogs and malteds from the vendor around the bend. Such an adult task! In "the box" our Dodger Dogs were hand-delivered by waiters in white coats. Pretty cool, but from our "regular" seats I could stand in line with the big people, carry money, show my stamped hand, which turned purple under the fluorescent light, to the guard, and return with all the

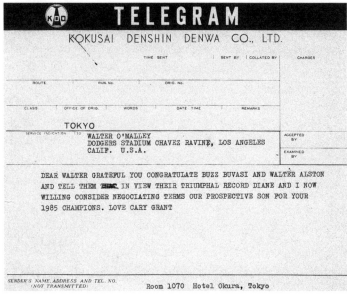

TELEGRAM

KOKUSAI DENSHIN DENWA CO., LTD.

TOKYO

WALTER O'MALLEY
DODGERS STADIUM CHAVEZ RAVINE, LOS ANGELES
CALIF. U.S.A.

DEAR WALTER GRATEFUL YOU CONGRATULATE BUZZ BUVASI AND WALTER ALSTON
AND TELL THEM ~~THAT~~ IN VIEW THEIR TRIUMPHAL RECORD DIANE AND I NOW
WILLING CONSIDER NEGOCIATING TERMS OUR PROSPECTIVE SON FOR YOUR
1985 CHAMPIONS. LOVE CARY GRANT

SENDER'S NAME, ADDRESS AND TEL. NO.
(NOT TRANSMITTED)   Room 1070 Hotel Okura, Tokyo

Dad's telegram to Dodgers owner Walter O'Malley. If I had been a boy,
perhaps I could have won them a pennant.

goodies. Much more fun. Occasionally, we still went to the owners' box for special events. Much to the O'Malleys' amusement, I taught Dad "the bump" during an Elton John concert. Dad stood stationary, waggling his hips back and forth while I jumped 180 degrees to bump hips from each side. Oh, he laughed.

IF BROWSING WAS the order of the day, Dad was drawn to the Fox Hills Mall. A somewhat bizarre departure from the normal Grant environs, Fox Hills was a huge, neon-lit, consumer-packed, hustle-bustle, gargantuan, hideous brown structure in Culver City. JC Penney was the top draw. This was no Beverly Hills, Santa Monica, or Century City. Even in the late seventies Fox Hills was ghetto. It was our first real experience with indoor shopping malls, and magically, Dad rarely tired of taking me there. Usually we'd just

Dad and bundle of Jennifer near the Santa Monica incline section of the Pacific Coast Highway. We're on the side patio of one of those extraordinary half-acre beach-front homes, in 1966.

meander together. Maybe grab some fast food or pop by the record store. Something about his Bristol upbringing lit up amid the bright lights, big city–ness of it. Semirobotically, Dad gazed around at all the vendors, blinking and nodding more than usual, as if registering what all this meant to society. Surprisingly, we could amble there. I guess the Fox Hills crowd wasn't looking for Cary Grant, because if people did recognize him, they mercifully let us be. The Brentwood Country Mart, a sweet, inviting red barn–like assembly of shops at the corner of Twenty-sixth and San Vicente, was another manageable, oft-strolled getaway. Normality for a glide through the mall. Bliss.

Who can blame the public for effectively squashing most of our private jaunts? Everyone wanted to be near Dad. People feel it's their right. After all, they've paid good money to sit and watch stars up close, for years. They've felt intimacy from within the cinema, and when the person comes to life in front of their eyes, I suppose the moth instinct just takes over. On the rare occasion we

Our ticket stub from a Father's Day Dodgers game spent in the O'Malleys' box. Dad's print reads: "Father's Day! Jennifer and Nurse Mimi and me in Walter O'Malley's box."

entered an off-the-beaten-path establishment (be it a gas station or a deli), looky loos hovered around us, fish-bowl style. Women were wide-eyed, hunched over, and giggly. Straight back to high school. Men gave sideways "I'm not really noticing you" glances. Dad gently kept his distance with a soft smile, polite nod, and constant forward motion. I found it annoying. I wanted Dad to myself.

Chapter Ten

Acting

Dad reached the top. The tippity top. Apex of the apex. I believe his success found its roots in play. Dad loved acting and he made work fun. It was an extension of the joy and playfully exuberant quality he had in life. Dad was a sweet, cunning, playful little devil. His charm captivated the world. Dad was who he was. He wasn't masking some inner discontent by playing the clown. He was a clown. There are many talented comedians whose verbal riffs and acerbic wit are admirable, but I rarely enjoy their performances. Their intellect is astute enough, and yet I feel slightly ill at ease watching them. My informed guess is that pain drives the performance. While one may appreciate sharp, glib commentary, the resonating emotion is still discomfort. Dad, on the other hand, was congruent with the comedy he portrayed. He shared from a place of abundance, and his gifts of laughter were felt through one's entire spirit. He laughed with, never at, you.

```
        BHB 132(0953)(1-099065G221)PD 08/09/78 0950
ICS IPMIIHA IISS
 IISS FM RCA 09 0950
PMS BEVERLYHILLS CA
WUD4557 FUR 153  ZWA248 XTH 192 970396A  0643
USNX CO MCMX 048
MONTECARLO 48/45 9 1635 AMPLIATION
MR CARY GRANT
9966 BEVERLY GROVE DRIVE
BEVERLYHILLSCALIFORNIE90210
TRULY DELIGHTED BY YOUR ACCEPTANCE TO ATTEND WITH
JENNIFER CIRCUS FESTIVAL SEVENTH TO ELEVENTH DECEMBER STOP
MANY THANKS FOR YOUR SPONTANEOUS B SUPPORT LOOKING FORWARD TO
 GREETING YOU AND SWEET DAUGHTER STOP ALL BEST WISHES STOP
  RAINIER
 COL  9966 90210
```

*Prince Rainier generally kept his cards close, but he melted a little
where Dad was concerned.*

In Dad's eyes, the world held innumerable sources for reverie.
Dad "got teary" (as he called it) at the beauty in life, be it the glaciers, a duck pond, whales in the Pacific, or the Empire State Building. By the time I came into my father's life, Dad was a crier. I don't
remember him ever crying out of sadness, though I know that he
did. When I was with him Dad cried for joy. I grew up thinking
that men cried, and it was beautiful. The national anthem went
straight to Dad's heart. He loved our country. America was, in his
estimation, the best place in the world. He was quite proud of his
citizenship. A free-market economy—"miraculous!" The right to
self-determination—"the best gift a man can have." He was childlike in his reverence for life's many gifts. Dad gaped, starry-eyed in
amazement, at the sight of Horowitz's fingers gliding over piano
keys or Baryshnikov leaping into the air. Dad particularly appreciated talent. He never lost the purity of heart it takes to lose oneself
in art.

· · ·

PEOPLE OFTEN SAY that Cary Grant "created himself." Well, don't we all? The comment is made disparagingly, as though Dad donned a mask for the world. Dad held up his ideals and stuck to them. Perhaps that's the distinction. Cary Grant successfully hit his character mark, whereas others forge theirs by default, or bemoan falling short.

Dad was tough on his work, particularly his early stuff. He literally couldn't watch some of his comedies. *Arsenic and Old Lace* made him shudder. WHY?! It's a hilarious, sweet, madcap, thoroughly memorable movie. "Egads, all the overwrought double takes, all the gags. . . . I'm way over the top." Yes. And it worked beautifully! It took him a few years to hone his less-is-more double takes. I'd argue there's room for both. Remember him prancing around in a woman's robe in *Bringing Up Baby*? His perfect horizontal leap when May Robson asks him why he's dressed that way? "Because I've just gone gay all of a sudden!" Nothing less would've done.

Dad didn't "get" acting classes. "If you want to act, get out there and do it. You'll never learn what it's like to be on a set when you're stuck in a classroom." He didn't sit around asking "how"; instead, Dad found a way. Now, others of us may need classes as a means of building the self-confidence to just get out there and do it. True to his Capricorn self, Dad trudged up the hill regardless of self-doubt. "On a set there are lights and sound and marks and all sorts of things to deal with. It's not all about "acting." He took the acting part for granted. Acting was easy for him. It was make-believe and he jumped in. The rest was the business.

By Dad's own admission, he wasn't a character actor. Meryl Streep, Dustin Hoffman, and Philip Seymour Hoffman are generally known for their brilliance in inhabiting a character's skin. They take what may be one tiny aspect of themselves and blow it up larger than life. Dad did something relatively opposite that; he played the same basic man, himself, and honed tiny aspects. Sure, in *Operation Petticoat* he was the able captain; in *To Catch a Thief,* the insouciant cat burglar John Robie. But his basic psychology remains fairly consistent throughout. He's generally unflappable and always charming, witty, and playful. He deals with opposition readily, discreetly, and efficiently. It's who he was as a man. It's fun to watch all types of actors, and all are needed. The craft one chooses most probably reflects an individual's aptitude and, therefore, highest method of self-expression.

If Dad had an acting theory, it was a respect for language and the body. Dad was a fan of enunciation. Some of it was the Brit in him: "It's *h*erbs, not 'erbs . . . *Au*-tomobile, not ottomobile, darling." His articulation was a mellifluous joy. Sharp voices "sent" him. "Modulate your voice" is a directive I'm quite familiar with. Dad also spoke highly of economic gestures: "Don't distract from what you're saying with your hands. . . . People who move their hands this way and that as they speak are really telling you that they don't wish to be heard." He liked my acting (pat pat on my own back) because I didn't flail around. I'd learned from years in his company not to reduce my words with unnecessary actions. The body speaks too.

He was quite proud of his Academy Award. It took the Academy until Dad's retirement to honor him with a lifetime achievement award. If you ask me, he deserved ten. Dad questioned why comedians and handsome men weren't honored as often as dramatic actors and, well, less handsome men. Are good looks their own reward, canceling out the right to more? My father never spoke of his own good looks. Occasionally he grumbled about his gray hair, and the additional five to ten pounds around his middle. Perhaps the Academy assuaged his ego with the award? He found the Academy biased. Dad admired Robert Redford—"It'll be tough for him to be awarded anything . . . he's just too good looking." One could of course cite examples of handsome, comedic actors winning "serious" awards, but by and large, it's a rare breed . . . and one that, when found, is, perhaps, underappreciated.

As far as his movies went, the policy stated: "If you're watching my movies, you're up too late at night. You could be doing something useful with your time, like sleeping." True, it was his modesty, but also true to the way he lived his life. Dad just didn't watch films. At all. His detachment from the medium that made him a huge star was almost weird. Most celebrities I know are "into" movies. They go along for the ride of the film and also deconstruct its business. Once retired, Dad gave it all up. No movies, no industry magazines, no showbiz chatter, and zero gossip. He admired "Grace" and "Hitch," but a bemused grin was as far as his recollections went. One would think I had a treasure trove of stories from his movie career. Not so. For whatever reason, we never discussed his life as an actor. He never told me of the many great directors, writers, and actors with whom he collaborated. How tremendously silly of me not to ask. Dad had been in it, but he was certainly not of it. To me, it's like renting horses after having owned them. Unfulfilling. Dad knew how to move on.

DAD HAD A SENSE of the apex. Perhaps his skill at comedy translated to life as well. He knew timing. There's a natural limit for everything. The height of an experience. Beyond the crest, it's all downhill. The way I translate it is, when you're at the top of your game . . . get out. Dad did that in his career. He also applied that philosophy to parties, concerts, sporting events, and conversations. Part of "getting out" had to do with good planning. If we left Dodger games at the top of the ninth, we'd avoid traffic. Another side to it was his sense of pride. It's akin to "always leave them wanting more," and, conversely, "always leave wanting more." Dad "retired" at his peak. He retired by choice. The offers still rolled in. Critics charged he was robbing the world of his talent too soon. He took it on the nose. Candidly, he joked that he didn't want to watch himself grow old on-screen. "Ah, vanity!" he'd say. The truth was, he couldn't work and devote his full attention to the child he wanted. In 1966, when I was born, my father retired from acting at age sixty-two. He had made his mark on the world; now it was time to make his mark as a father. With his signature, singular devotion, he dove in.

The world misses my father's movies and so do I. I'm continually questing for that giddy, yearn-inducing, ticklish moviegoing experience. Alas, the popcorn generally provides my biggest thrill. I sadly agree with A. O. Scott's Sunday *New York Times* article decrying the state of modern romances:

"In general the trough of late winter and early spring is Hollywood's designated season of mediocrity. . . . Our parents and grandparents had Rock Hudson and Doris Day, such delicious subtext! . . . Spencer Tracy and Katharine Hepburn. Or Katharine Hepburn and Cary Grant. Or Cary Grant and Rosalind Russell . . . while the romantic comedy has almost always trafficked in happy endings, that happiness is rarely accompanied by a sense of risk or exhilaration. When you think of, say, Cary Grant and Katharine Hepburn . . . you recall the emotional combat of two strong willed, independent individuals ending in mutual conquest. Love, in those old pictures, was a dangerous and noble sport that required skill and cunning as well as commitment. It required movie stars whose physical appeal was matched by verbal dexterity and a vital sense of idiosyncrasy."

Dad made me aware that not everyone's father had his own airplane, with his initials in the registration number, N396CG. Still, the magnificence of it all didn't dawn on me until many years later. Circa 1971.

We crave that idiosyncratic romantic comedy bliss. There may not be any Cary Grant clones out there, but there are certainly gifted, witty, agile, confident, handsome, charming, winsome men in the world . . . aren't there?

The single movie I remember Dad seeing was *Silver Streak*. We had a date to go to the Malibu Cinemas for an evening of comedy. Laugh till we cried time. Thereafter, Dad was thoroughly enamored with Gene Wilder and Richard Pryor. Dad enjoyed the clean humor and physical comedy. When they screened the movie aboard one of our Alaskan cruises, we went to see it a second time. This time, knowing the gags ahead of time, we laughed before, during, and after.

Dad's time on movie sets was etched in him. The way Dad recorded me and our goings-on at home had a cinematic quality to them. He was so accustomed to being seen, photographed, and recorded, it was second nature for him to have an outside observer to life. One typewritten, aged, browned piece of paper found among the archives and titled "JENNIFER SNAPSHOTS" reads just like a script supervisor's notes. In the margins he wrote asides. At the top of the page, in his own print, "Jennifer wrote Grant for the first time on 3rd November 1969." He generally wrote descriptions of each

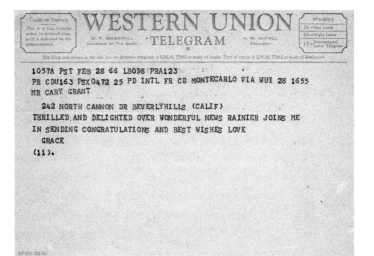

Princess Grace's congratulatory telegram to Dad on my birth. A simple glance from Princess Grace had the power and focus to make me feel special.

A restaurant in New York, 1969. (Note the woman gleefully peering over at us.)

color photograph on the reverse side. Dad describes one color photo of baby Jennifer on the floor with glasses as "The week of January 23–29, 1967, with my spectacles. Dear Jennifer was always fascinated with my spectacles."

THERE'S A SIMPLE EXPLANATION for why people feel close to movie stars. In many ways we are. Some characters are intimately linked with the actor. In revealing their characters' strengths, weaknesses, delights, faults, foibles, and oddities, they reveal themselves. To illustrate: Dad undoubtedly improvised some of *Father Goose*'s Walter Eckland. It's fun to witness the seldom seen side of Cary Grant. His rough, gruff, negotiating, rapscallion self. While Leslie Caron instructs a group of schoolgirls on the finer points of etiquette for a deserted island, Dad admonishes, "Why don't you teach them something useful . . . like catching a fish?" There's the Dad I know! "Are you sure you want to go to Stanford, Jennifer? You could get a job instead. . . . Perhaps I've done you a disservice by leaving you money . . . you always have something to fall back on. Will you be motivated to work for a living?" Good questions.

Clearly, business fascinated Dad. "I've wasted my time being an actor. I should've been out there in the world studying things. Economics is what it's all about." In truth, Dad never really considered another career. He did fancy the idea of being a conductor. "Imagine standing up there in front of an orchestra . . . what a wonderful feeling." Besides Hollywood Park, Dad was on the board of MGM and Fabergé. Thanks to his profitable career, Dad could devote himself to nonpaying jobs and let the horizontal money roll in. "Horizontal money" was Dad's favored cash. Quincy Jones introduced the term. "Horizontal money" . . . that's what we want. It's the money you make while you're sleeping. You do nothing vertically to produce it. It just rolls right on in. Dad howled at the mention of "horizontal money."

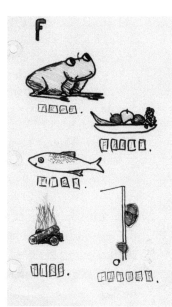

A page out of Dad's handmade-for-Jennifer "Alphabet Book," circa 1972. Here we have the F's: frogs, fruit, fish, fire, and father.

As far as money goes, I've heard ridiculous rumors exaggerating our family's wealth, and others debunking Dad as "tight with a buck." In my experience, Dad was neither cheap nor excessive. Which, for a wealthy man, is remarkable. He was educated about value and unencumbered by greed. This note to his friend, the top-notch fabulous florist Harry Finley, shows that Dad wasn't afraid to address the subject of worth head-on. No false pride about it.

Thank you, Harry,
    Your flowers are attractive and colorful; but then so are you, my friend. Still, since I customarily send flowers prior to attending a dinner party I'm often enabled to see the arrangements too, and

learned that other florists also sent attractive and colorful baskets but for considerably lower prices. So, because, like you, I am a businessman and take into consideration the proximity of the florist, freshness of flowers, size and similarity of comparative baskets, plus addition (or deletion) of delivery charges, my wife and I decided to experiment elsewhere. And "that" as Lilly Tomlin so effectively says, "is the TRUTH."

Nevertheless Harry, our friendship will, I trust, continue quite happily as before.

Cary

In his later years, sensing death's approach, Dad apologized to me several times for not focusing more on finances. "You know, if I'd stuck around acting I could have made a lot more dough for you." He meant it. He wanted to give me the world. In his total devotion, he did.

Chapter Eleven

Fame

What's it like to be the daughter of a "star"? If I've heard the question once ... There's no general answer. Celebrities share some basic similarities, but I'd wager that there are just as many differences. Stars are like Ben & Jerry's ice cream. Lots of flavorful choices and no place for bland. I grew up around actors, writers, directors, and all the facets of the Hollywood world—publicists, stylists, scripts, trainers, and so on. If six degrees of separation holds true, celebrity status brings the "upper echelons" of society closer to one's doorstep. Having a "name" naturally confers privilege. At least it gets you through many doors. Once inside, it's up to you. Dad used to say that if I chose acting as a career, he'd have no idea how to help me. The people he knew were at his level, the top. Dad had an ingrained belief that you work your way up. Earning it is the important part. He wanted me to know the value of achievement. The feeling of doing it on my own. There's a concept in Kabbalah called the bread of shame. Basically, it says if you're given something you haven't earned, you never internalize its worth and it actually works against you. That's the veritable obstacle of being born into celebrity. If one's down, the pressure of celebrity is like swimming with ankle weights in a ten-foot swell. Luckily, if one breaks the surface, once up for air, there are nifty hovercrafts nearby.

Some things you learn only in Hollywood. I once made a little booboo with an AFI screen. Mom was directing a short for the women directors' series. *Number One* went on to win her an Academy Award nomination. While Mom edited her gem, my girlfriend Lisa and I did homework in an adjacent screening room. God knows what possessed me, but at some point I kissed the screen. Actually walked up and planted my lips on the silvery surface. Oops . . . I had some lip gloss on. Rub that right away. Oops again. That just smeared my kiss. Oh dear, better stop there. It was as obvious as an ink stain. A small scene ensued until AFI forgave Mom and Mom forgave us.

There are some amusingly tender spots to the whole "child of" thing. One must develop a keen eye for suck-ups and stay honest with personal motivations. Are relationships based on mutual respect or ego gratification? The glossy flame of fame attracts moths. Moths are low on Darwin's ladder. A few years back, a friend made me a proposition. Nearing my big fortieth birthday, he thought perhaps I wanted a child—"You know, I'd be happy to father a child with you." This is a pretty cool guy. . . . That's a big offer. . . . I must be pretty cool, too. Then, leaning back in his chair, staring up at the ceiling, he mused, "Imagine that, Cary Grant and I making a baby." Red flag. He was missing someone in the equation. Stunned, I somehow whimpered, "Thanks." Fame's shadow casts a wide net when vulnerabilities knock one off point.

It's a bizarre thing, particularly as a young child, to decipher what your parent is doing up on-screen acting like a different person in a fabricated incarnation of "Daddy." He never once asked me to

February 26, 1977

Dad's note to me on my eleventh birthday. Some people wait a lifetime to hear these words from parents. Luckily, Dad's effusive love must have erased my many selfish moments.

~~~
nnifer, dearest,

 are eleven years old today and are about to embark
 the second ten years of a wonderful life.

   Ten years have passed by since I first saw your
  face. Ten years. Ten years of loving you. Ten
 s of regarding you, of thinking of you, and of
 g with you at every opportunity possible to me.
 hose ten years you and I have shared the kind of
  and companionship I could not have shared with
 ne else.

   I am proud to know you. Proud to be seen with
   Proud and happy while watching you swim, ride,
 play tennis; and in each of our activities to-
 er: the Baseball games, the Races, every day at
 nhorn Ranch, the Malls; Everything; Everywhere.
  admiring of, and deeply affected by, your man-
  your kindness, and each new accomplishment. I
 ect your quiet loyalty to your friends and to
  of your parents.
~~~

CARY GRANT

You may have noticed that most of the previous
sentences begin with "I". Yet they could not begin with "I" if it weren't for YOU. You are the
dearest daughter a man could have. You have never
caused me a moment's anguish or disappointment.
Your qualities are of the best, and if you persist
in those qualities throughout life, you will enjoy
ever-growing happiness and, by so doing, understand the happiness you bring to others who know
you. Especially to me,

*Your father,
who loves you.*

TO JENNIFER,
ON THE TWENTY-SIXTH
OF FEBRUARY,
NINETEEN HUNDRED AND
SEVENTY SEVEN.

view one of his movies. It wasn't something we did. No Cary Grant fests for us. One exception occurred when I was three or four. We were in Westhampton, in our friends' den, where a group had assembled to watch *An Affair to Remember.* When Dad kissed Deborah Kerr I instantly popped off the couch and marched over to the television set. My young cheeks flushed with rage as I slapped the vixen's screen cheek. That got a big laugh. No stranger had the right to make out with my father! Maybe it happened in real life but not in front of me.

How does it feel to see my father on-screen? It's mostly squeamishly uncomfortable. Admittedly, I beam with pride and laugh out loud. However, there he was for all those years . . . doing all these amazing things, and I wasn't there with him. Grace Kelly gets to swim in the sea with him. I'm a good swimmer. That should be me. Katharine Hepburn flusters him. I could do that. Tony Curtis is an impertinent rascal. That's my job! If I yell loud enough, will he pop out of the screen for me? My Daddy, my Daddy, mine mine mine!!!! Okay, it's possible to intellectually delineate between his screen persona and who he was as my father, but that's part of the problem. This isn't the man I knew. Sure, many aspects are similar, but decades ago, he was a different man. He was most often wearing the bachelor hat. What? Daddy a bachelor? My daddy doesn't stay out late or go to parties or canoodle with Grace Kelly. He's too busy reading with me and swinging my dollies on tissue paper swings and filming my riding lessons. The cat burglar on-screen left his home without looking back—not my Dad! All rationalism takes flight. Funny. With Mom, the roles coexisted, Mom and funny woman in *Heaven Can Wait,* or Mom and disgruntled wife in *Honeysuckle Rose. . . .* It was easier to be comfortable with these characters because I watched them come to life in her and felt part of the world of those movies. Dad's acting career was in no way linked to our home life. It's something like knowing a mate's exes. They exist, but come on, is it actually necessary to hang out with them?

My parents were stars, yes, and ultimately, of course, stars are just people. So, stars or not, they were my parents. I was blessed with love from two parents.

When Dad picked me up at school, I saw Dad, the guy who plays me Tchaikovsky's *Sleeping Beauty* before I go to bed and Dad who takes me on after-school jaunts to survey Barbies at the Country Mart. Where others saw Cary Grant . . . I saw Dad. However, to some extent every little girl sees Daddy as Cary Grant. The difference was, in my case, Dad had already reached iconic status, so, as a little girl, the world mirrored the way I saw him. I guess that's what still pisses me off about seeing him in films. There he is, the star, Cary Grant. Everyone is able to retain that part. The part of him they knew still exists.

Okay, I had a crush on Dad. Okay, more than a little crush on Dad. My other, *real* crushes were Donny Osmond and Jean-Paul Belmondo. Crushes are a mandatory rite of passage, and my picks were the rosy-cheeked pure American boy and the French Cheshire cat. Dad watched from the living-room couch as my girlfriends and I dramatically gesticulated our lip-synched rendition of "Puppy Love" from the LP. Years later, I was a guest on Donny's talk show. "You mean, you sang 'Puppy Love' to Cary Grant?" He ate it up. Cary Grant was the man of women's dreams, but come on, to me he was still Dad. Donny Osmond was puppy love. People inside the gates still get starry-eyed. Maybe we're all part moth, like it or not. Jean-Paul Belmondo, one of Mom's costars on *Le casse,* was my first wobbly knees, deer-in-the-headlights experience. I was five. All I wanted to do was be near him and stare. My ploy—to temporarily chum up his Jack Russell terrier. Perfect. While Mom and Jean-Paul were acting I could play with the pooch. We were practically married! Maybe that explains French as my language of choice in grade school.

Chapter Twelve
Fame, the Lifestyle

Fame is a school of sorts. The University of Fame may be daunting. There is a varied curriculum with minors, majors, levels of mastery, and often complicated rules of negotiation. One will be faced with diversions and interruptions of every sort. No one knows exactly what to expect with fame. One arrives for the first time and the world takes on new hues. The difference for me is that fame was my birthright. Whatever degree of fame I have comes from my parents. Fame was a natural part of life. It was a day-to-day reality. We were a famous family. Simple as that. We ate, we slept, we drove a station wagon, we were famous. All part of life. But fame has its own list of attendant details.

Stars are great at getting where they want to go. Life is like a fish bowl out there on the road. You become instant "bubble people," stared at and pondered from all angles. This necessitates strategic, proactive mapping. Dad had the routing system wired. Mom still does. Perhaps it's a prerequisite to stardom that one appreciates special attention and enjoys calculating the route. Routes. Routes to everything. One of the major perks of celebrity is outrageous seats to sporting events. Sometimes it means shelling out big bucks, but more often it's a catch-22—once you've got the money, everything is suddenly free. Stars are magnets for attention, so, like advertising dollars, their presence pays for the gifted seat. Dad and I frequented Hollywood Park and Dodgers games. Mom's a huge Lakers fan. Getting to games means stepping into the efficiency zone. There are ingenious methods to avoid traffic that crisscross every major artery. Waiting just isn't a part of the game plan. It's somewhat awe-inspiring. Where mere mortals beep their horns on a clogged 405 freeway, Mom and Dad always wended their way through, virtually obstacle-free. Once there, all valets are familiar faces. In the time it takes to say, "Welcome back, Mr. Grant," the car is whisked away. No valet ticket.

There is a science to celebrity outings. To enjoy an excursion with Dad, we had to be prepared. Never tarry. The shortest distance between two points is a straight line. Focus. Strategize your entrances and exits. When socializing, warn the host in advance that you may "duck out early."

Our L.A. restaurant choices were Madame Wu's and La Scala Beverly Hills. I'm referring to the old La Scala, on the corner of Rodeo and Santa Monica. There, we'd be led to "the back booth," around the corner, so Dad wasn't glanced from the door. Otherwise the entire meal became a gape fest. When I grew up Dad was done with schmoozing. We went out, once every few weeks, for the sake of a good meal. Getting out was never to meet people we didn't know. On the contrary, usually it meant staying away from people we didn't know. I once dated someone well-known who made painstaking efforts to visit with every fan who crossed his path. Trouble was, it took us literally hours to get through the supermarket. The fans were thrilled, but I'd had it. If Dad and I did get stuck in a crowd, he would gently remind autograph seekers, "I'm sorry, I

Dad's letter to me on my semester at sea voyage. I remember feeling terribly homesick on this trip — the distance felt enormous. Gemma (our then cook and housekeeper, mentioned at bottom), works for Barbara and her husband, David Jaynes, and on occasion for me and baby Cary, to this happy day.

just can't do it or we would start a chain reaction and I'd be here all day." I've heard that phrase literally thousands of times.

Occasionally, we had the odd bit of "night life." One of our old Hollywood haunts was the private Magic Castle. A subculture of Hollywood magicians performing in a veritable castle club. Dinner and a show. The food is not the main attraction. The close-up room, where card tricks are performed virtually under your nose, completely flummoxed Dad. "How do they *do* that? . . . Marvelous." In Las Vegas, Dad snuck me into the adult shows to see great magicians. With the patrons buzzing and the lights dimmed, we'd work our way into the showroom after the opening showgirl act, and slink

The divine feeling of leaning back and trusting Dad. Place and origin unknown, circa 1970.

out before closing. It bothered Dad that children were banned from revues. "For God's sake . . . they're breasts! . . . She'll have some eventually!" Dad was kicked out of grade school for peeping-tom behavior. The adolescent Archie was hoisting me up onto the locker room fence with him!

MOM AND DAD socialized me early. I went along to parties, clubs, and fetes. If the environment was okay for them, it was okay for me, too. Neither of them were big night people. Mom took me with her to "adult" dinner parties, where generally I found a comfy couch to curl up on and sleep. The concept of "getting out there," socializing, and meeting people to make one's way up the business ladder still confounds me. It never occurred to me that people actually had to leave their homes to socialize. Most of "the powers that be" came to our house. Still, business was business, socializing was socializing. We never sat around a dinner table and talked business. Somehow in my mind, business just happened. It was what one did during the day. Mom went to the set. Dad worked as a director on boards. The work just came to them. That's how I saw it.

Getting out there on my own was at first a rude awakening.

My childhood experience with celebrity and inherent fame left me entirely ill-prepared for the realities of the world. Elite college and boarding school are philosophical bubbles. Celebrity life is a societal bubble. I was bubble girl and my many worlds popped when I stepped out on my own. All the good grades and good intentions aside, wrangling with life from the bottom up makes no sense when you're used to looking at things from the top down. Growing up as a "have," envy is a far-off concept. Most of my friends had plenty, too. I was used to sharing the wealth as a way of life. Alligator briefcase falls hard. Let's just say I've been through some paradigm shifts since childhood.

Dad carried his fame lightly. When I was in my teens Dad was in his seventies. He was accustomed to handling the limelight and did it with ease. What did he use when times got tough? Common sense, I suppose. He was not a religious man. His spiritual nature is best summed up by his favorite "meditation" (author unknown):

Now Lord, you've known me for a long time. You know me better than I know myself. You know that each day I am growing older and someday may even be very old, so meanwhile please keep me from the habit of thinking I must say something on every subject and on every occasion.

Release me from trying to straighten out everyone's affairs. Make me thoughtful, but not moody, helpful, but not overbearing. I've a certain amount of knowledge to share; still it would be very nice to have a few friends who, at the end, recognized and forgave the knowledge I lacked.

Keep my tongue free from the recital of endless details. Seal my lips on my aches and pains: They increase daily and the need to speak of them becomes almost a compulsion. I ask for grace enough to listen to the retelling of others' afflictions, and to be helped to endure them with patience.

I would like to have improved memory, but I'll settle for growing humility and an ability to capitulate when my memory clashes with the memory of others. Teach me the glorious lesson that on some occasions I may be mistaken.

Keep me reasonably kind; I've never aspired to be a saint . . . saints must be rather difficult to live with. . . . Yet, on the other hand, an embittered old person is a constant burden.

Please give me the ability to see good in unlikely places and talents in unexpected people. And give me the grace to tell them so, dear Lord.

While fame held up a glossy picture for the world, Dad's inner life was a disciplined and gently reflective domain.

Chapter Thirteen

Society of Gossips — or,
Mind Your Own Business

In the early seventies, Dad and I lived at 92 Malibu Colony. Or
was it 91? 90 perhaps? The miscalculation could mean a huge
difference to someone's monthlies. One might imagine affected
Realtors shuffling off to the courthouse to look up public housing
records or some such thing. Mom and I also lived in the Colony. We
lived at number 98. That one's for sure. One Halloween many years
later, I trick-or-treated in the Colony. Our former home had been
redone and then reredone. Curious, I asked 98's new owners for a
peek. They allowed me and only me into the house. *Merde, alors.* Our
formerly avant-garde Moroccan home had been turned into a pastel
nightmare. The owner enlightened me about Mom and Dad living
in the master for years. How did I miss that? No. Simply not true at
all. Had the Realtor sold the house on this premise? Perhaps Dad

had also lived here with his gay lovers? Another night I was at Malibu Cinemas, and I overheard the woman in front of me discussing her friendship with Cary Grant's son, my brother. I wanted to know my brother, too. Did he live with me? How old was he? Was he younger or older than I? Could he protect me and introduce me to all of his cute friends? Maybe Mom and Dad had him during all those years they were living together in that room at 98. My point is . . . where there's smoke . . . sometimes it's just a poisonous cigarette.

FAME — THE PRICE

It's awkward living with public misconceptions about my father. What does one say when asked if one's famously charming, debonair, five-times-married, crooned-over father is gay? Hmmm . . . a grin escapes me. Can't blame men for wanting him, and wouldn't be surprised if Dad even mildly flirted back. If so, it manifested as witty repartee as opposed to a pat on the ass. That's a sign of healthy, secure sexuality. Isn't it remarkable that in this day and age anyone would seek to impugn Dad's character with a hint at homosexuality. Being gay is neither here nor there, but hiding oneself from family and friends . . . not so good. When the question arises, it generally speaks more about the person asking. Of course, Dad somewhat enjoyed being called gay. He said it made women want to prove the assertion wrong. When asked if Dad was gay, Betsy Drake had the best answer: "I don't know, we were always too busy fucking for me to ask."

The gay rumor normally seemed funny to Dad. All but once. I don't remember the exact situation, but I do remember Dad raising his voice. A blessedly unfamiliar occurrence. Chevy Chase made some joke about Dad being gay. Why? Whatever Mr. Chase's personal baggage, it's just sad when curiosity turns from speculation to jab. Particularly within the ranks.

Perhaps Dad's maverick nature coupled with his grace were simply difficult to categorize. Perhaps Dad had what Virginia Woolf described as an "androgynous mind." She asks "whether there are two sexes in the mind corresponding to the two sexes in the body and whether they also require to be united in order to get complete satisfaction and happiness . . . a great mind is androgynous. It is when this fusion takes place that the mind is fully fertilized and uses all its faculties. . . . The androgynous mind is resonant and porous; it transmits emotion without impediment; that it is naturally creative, incandescent and undivided." Well, that's a mouthful. Easier to just call him gay. Perhaps if minds were more androgynous there would be less prejudice, less bigotry, and less hatred.

All the homosexual speculation begs another question. Did Dad ever experiment sexually? I don't know. Have I ever experimented sexually? Have you? If experimentation makes one gay, then my guess is that most of the world is gay.

When did it become okay for us to snoop, to pry, to prod, to invade privacy? Dad was an actor, not a politician. I'm not sure it's okay to interlope behind the closed doors of politicians' lives, either, but there seems to be a more relevant argument for it. Politicians espouse some moral position in ruling. Their lives should therefore mirror their assertions, and it's valuable to know if they're debasing themselves by holding a double standard. With actors, at least, shouldn't we be able to judge by how we're affected? If performances move us, isn't that enough? By prying, we only reveal our trustlessness. We don't trust ourselves to feel. When we feel, when some example helps us go deep and stirs up some pain, we want to slaughter the icon. In so doing, we curtail the growth that might emerge from grace. Interloping became sanctioned when we started buying tabloids, in any form.

I've always had a "yech" response to tabloids. Where's the love? It's one thing to project onto stars . . . that's part of the game. It's expected the way a therapist or teacher might expect to be distorted to meet any given student's needs. But tabloids seem to be more of a cultural thermometer. What are we getting away with as a society? What are our most minute and grandest flaws and who can we "catch" at them. Who looks grossly fat? Who's got cancer? Who's heart is broken? Who had a bad hair day and needs to be outed for it? It's as if we're testing our own ability to cope with freedom. Famous people have earned a certain freedom, and with it comes the temptation of excess of every sort. There's the money, the power, the drugs, the sex, the alcohol, the food, the shopping, the possibility of excessing. So . . . let's put a magnifying glass on these people and see if they implode. Well, of course some do, some have, and some will.

I'm grateful to actors for putting themselves up there on the big screen for us to gawk at. I learn from movies. Isn't being an example on-screen enough? Can we learn through stories, through parables? Take them to our heart and be grateful that someone has the courage to get up there for us and be emotionally truthful, so that we heal ourselves? Or learn by example what path to avoid? An actor is an actor. They're telling us a story. That's it. Their lives should be their private territory, unless they want to talk about it.

If it takes übercontrol to forge a successful name and career, then it's a dark trick that once there, one must relinquish that image for public consumption. Several years back a soft drink company used old film clips of Dad's image to promote their sugary crap. Dad hated soft drinks. Particularly this one. When I was five or so years old, he poured a glass of that particular dark brown carbonated sugary soda and placed my baby tooth in it. Then Dad and I watched my tooth disintegrate. Dad spent his life creating himself, honoring his values, and in five minutes some soft drink company found it permissible to use Cary Grant's image to sell their chemical poison to the world. That's a fiasco. In 2007, Jimi Hendrix was being used to promote a new energy drink. Jimi, I don't know if you drank cola and I don't really care. I still promise never to buy the ill-begotten product that they purport you represent.

As a child, on the odd occurrence, I was sad to see my parents unfairly lambasted by the press. Later it made me angry. Now my

*Willie Watson, circa
1973. Not a false bone
in her body.*

skin has thickened a bit. The motto "Soul of a rose, hide of an ele-
phant" works especially well in Hollywoodland.

My favorite nanny, Willie Watson, put it best with her sage
advice about people: "Don't you pay them no nevermind. You let
other people do what they're going to do. You mind your own business." That heals almost as well as her Southern chocolate cake with
powdered sugar in the frosting.

PAPARAZZI. Hmm. Mom and Dad always kept me as far away
from photo hounds as possible. Mostly, I had an easy time around it.
When the freewheeling press descended it was like some bizarre
flood of light in the face, cameras sticking into the car windows,
people calling our names . . . a wave of frenzied flashes. The only
time it became gravely disconcerting was after Dad's death. Finals
time at Stanford and, two weeks after his death, I chose to get on
with the program. There would be plenty of time to let it soak in.
Plenty of time to mourn. Keeping up with my work and focusing on
school would help me cope. Stay with my classmates. As I did my

dailies around campus, the paparazzi trailed me a few times by car. Having had stalkers in my life, being followed is just creepy. The first time I tried to ditch whoever it was who was following me, the person in the passenger seat aimed his large telephoto lens at me. My heart skipped a beat. Thinking it was a gun, I ducked under my own steering wheel. Luckily I didn't crash in the middle of El Camino Real. I raced back to my apartment, where they snapped a picture of me in the driveway. Must say, while Mom and Dad were at the helm, they made every effort to shield me from unnecessary exposure. They cherished my privacy and my right to choose.

My father had a zero tabloid mentality. Dad was into the thoughtful detail, the refined idea. The exact opposite of shock for shock value. Okay, bold colors are fun. If life needed a bit of a pick-me-up, CG could add splash in his wardrobe instead of filling his brain with muck. A Chinese red button-down shirt perhaps. Pow! Pizzazz! Immediate gratification of the urge to splurge.

Perhaps Dad's reputation is as glowing as it is because he chose to celebrate life, and celebrate himself as a lucky participant in life, instead of expecting life to celebrate him. Dad didn't want a funeral. "Funerals are for the living, not the dead. The dead are dead. If you would like to do something for me, please scatter my ashes over the ocean. Place me into infinity. Have Kirk go along, if you please." Same theory and practice for weddings. "It's an intimate action, it needs an intimate ceremony. Is my aunt's second cousin's nephew part of the marriage? If so, waaaatch out!" We never once had a big birthday party for Dad. He didn't want one. Christmas, okay . . . livitup! It's a group thing . . . everyone's included. At my birthday parties, Dad insisted that we give each guest their own gift to open. "What . . . they're all just going to sit there and watch you open your presents? Fat chance department!" Rarely was Dad taken to task by the press. When he was, he ignored it. Dad received and still receives almost entirely glowing reviews of every sort. He got what he deserved.

The challenge of being Dad's daughter has very little to do with stardom. It has to do with making the most of my life, of myself. Dad believed in one life, no reincarnation. You do what you do and then you're gone. Make it count.

Nap time. Daddy has a bit of a cold.

JG: Do you love me, Daddy?
CG: I love you very much.
JG: We won't be able to go to sleep if . . .
CG: We have everything we want. We have food and a good book . . . and I have you and we have love.

Jennifer picks "magic fur" off her Winnie-the-Pooh doll and rubs it on Daddy's head to make him feel good. Daddy rubs the magic fur on Jennifer's head, too.

Chapter Fourteen
Mom & Dad—Mad at the Cookies

JULY 7, 1966 · ABOARD SS *ORIANA*

Mom, Dad, and infant Jennifer.

Mom: Come on, darling. Put this leg over, darling. That was a good girl. . . . She turned over.
Dad: Oh my gosh, she's doing it. She's crawling.

Jennifer breathes with effort as both parents encourage her along the cabin bed's eiderdown comforter.

The early days. Viewing the earliest photos, the precious few with Mom, Dad, and me together, melts me. We're all happy. Well, I'm an infant . . . so it's hard to tell exactly how I felt as the pictures were taken, but the process of viewing them is certainly a happy one. We were still a family. An American dream. My father, a hand-

One of my favorite pictures of Mom, circa 1967. The summer hat, the dignified gaze . . . gorgeous.

some man, my mother, an astoundingly beautiful woman, and me. They both look so joyous. Their focus, however, in all of the pictures, is on their baby. Never on each other. There's something about having your parents on either side of you, together. I've never really understood that. I can see it here.

Something in me has always felt that my parents came together to make me. Vanity? Perhaps. Of course, they had love for each other. However, it's doubtful that either of them truly believed they'd stay together. Mom and Dad were and are headstrong beings. Both, in my opinion, need to rule the roost. While their ideals were similar, their personal expressions were quite different. The disparity has left me with a fairly open mind, and one that can tolerate the friction necessary for growth. Though their mixed beliefs were challenging to sort out as a child, I'm now happy for their dissimilarities.

Mom and Dad divorced when I was about a year old. Both parents encouraged me to love the other: "Don't be afraid to love your mother" and "It's okay to love your father." We never discussed their marriage. Their love. Their good stuff. I see it in the pictures and hear it on the tapes, but miragelike, it's untouchable. Dad's hand-written description of an early snapshot of the three of us reads, "Sunday evening, July 10, 1966. In Cabin of SS *Oriana* before a gala champagne carnival party." That sounds fun. Who wouldn't have fun at a "gala champagne carnival party"? Especially looking the way they looked. I'm a little nugget bundle wrapped in blue velour. Mom's a stunner in her sequined gown. It certainly appears that they're keeping the romance alive. What was on their minds? Your guess is as good as mine. In a pre–Jennifer era photo, Mom sits under an umbrella on the patio at 9966, at what looks like tea-time. She has a bob haircut and wears a Jackie O–style sleeveless dress. Oh, to be a fly on that wall. To see them court each other. Granted, Mom and Dad had their hard times. They divorced. But what brought them together? I missed that part. We can be so stu-pid in love. It's like diets. It's hard to stop after one potato chip, so we don't eat any. During my thoroughly preposterous teen dieting phase, Grandma would taunt me with her mouthwatering rugelach. "What, you don't like the cookies?" "*No!* Of course I like the cook-ies. I love the cookies. But I can't look at the cookies for fear of eat-ing eight of them, so let's grind them up in the disposal." I couldn't simply like the cookies. Mom and Dad couldn't simply like each other. Their chemistry was a disservice to their friendship. Mom and Dad were mad at the cookies.

As a child, my time was split between Mom and Dad. Mom had more time with me, but due to her thriving career, I spent plenty of time at Dad's. If Mom went away for a few months to do a movie while my schooling needed to continue in L.A., I stayed with Dad. Sort of complicated, but it all worked out. The weeknights that Mom was in town, I spent at her house, but Monday afternoon and evening were with Dad. That's where the root beer float tradition comes in. In my sixth-grade year Dad and I discovered that the Mal-ibu A&W stand had terrific root beer floats. Every Monday he'd pick me up at Carden Malibu School on Las Flores Canyon and drive

PCH up the coast to A&W. The A&W stand had a huge plaster man on top of it. The man was twice as large as the stand. When the stand changed to a Mexican place the man got a sombrero, but I still see him as the A&W guy. If you drive down PCH, he's still there. Dad and I would get our root beer floats and then sometimes just sit in the car talking and enjoying our treats. Other Mondays we'd drive over to the Colony Mart and amble along window-shopping. I might pretend to really want something in the window of the shoe store. A pair of "corkies," the cork-heeled wedge platforms that my parents forbade me, were perfect Dad bait. Maybe I could get him all riled up about the preposterous style, or the danger, or the ludicrous thought of me wearing corkies at twelve or thirteen. Of course, I never cared about the shoes. It was all about getting a rise out of Dad.

In many ways my parents flipped roles. Dad played more of the traditional mom; Mom, the traditional dad. When I was at Dad's, he took full charge of my care. We had a house staff, but they never took responsibility for me. Dad awakened me each morning, drove me everywhere, ate meals with me, discussed life with me, and tucked me in each evening. Don't get me wrong. He didn't stifle me by watching my every move. I had plenty of time alone. Being an only child, time alone is built into the deal. Mom had a full-fledged movie career when I was a child. Still, what I saw was Mom, the person who made sure I wore my retainer at night, or Mom, the woman who made me drink my milk . . . and if I was lucky added Quik powdered chocolate to it. What I didn't see was Mom, the woman who had just worked sixteen-hour days for a relentless director, or Mom who was just nominated for an Academy Award. I remember visiting movie sets and seeing her countless letters from others. Being a star is quite a balancing act. Dad had done his time on sets, now it was time to play at home. So as Mom was out "bringing home the bacon," Dad and I made bacon at home.

In large part, Mom and Dad were comically different. Mom eats fruit, nuts, vegetables, fish and chicken, zero red meat, and little wheat or sugar. Dad was into anything fatty and swore off fruit almost entirely. Mom is a hippie at heart. She listened to rock and roll, pop, Aretha and Stevie, and dressed in tie-dye, denim, and boots. Dad was the noted, timeless classicist. Horowitz or Sinatra, flannel, cashmere, and loafers. Mom's known for her happily raucous, attention-getting laugh. Dad modulated his voice to keep attention away.

Okay, they shared some similar quirks. Dad had his own candy stash. Mom did too. The difference was, Mom hid all the candy from herself. Actually, she had a lock put on the cabinet and gave me the key. Being a self-disciplined child and because Mom allowed me sugar, I never went overboard with what we called the kaka cupboard. The only thing off-limits was giving her the key. This wasn't always easy. On the flip side, Dad's sweets were his and his alone. You didn't go in the goody drawer without permission. Mom's kaka cupboard and Dad's goody drawer. They were both literally trying to control the cookies.

While Dad held demure soirees at 9966, Mom threw beach bashes at 98. Mom's parties meant lots of people, music, and mayhem. It was one of the few occasions when Mom cooked. Barbecue spareribs were her specialty. That and curried chicken salad. I liked to help Mom cook for parties. One year, upon completion of three virtual vats of our famous chicken salad, we discovered that Mom's finger was missing its Band-Aid. *Merde.* We never found it. Nevertheless, watchful-eyed, we served the curried treat. Luckily, no one reported the bonus Band-Aid. My guess is that the poor soul must have imbibed Mom's magical melon concoction prior to eating. Mom would halve a watermelon, scoop out the insides, fill it with various liquors, and add melon balls to the solution. This generally produced wild bongo drum sessions in the living room. Mom's good on drums. Her signature lioness curly blond locks flew as she beat out the rhythm. The living room turned tribal at music time. I was tambourine queen. As if we stepped right out of the musical *Hair.* "Let the sun shine" and all that.

Mom was never a moderate gal. Why have a bite of ice cream when we bought a quart? Dad wore moderation like the tuxes that suited him "just so." I suppose I fall somewhere between my mother and father. Constitutionally, I'm ill-suited for debauchery. When I smoked, I smoked one or two cigarettes a day. Mom's atypical, but effective, response to my disgusting behavior: "Oh honey, that's child's play. . . . Really . . . how do you do that? I used to smoke at least a pack and a half. You must suck in one or two just walking around L.A." That took the oomph right out of my sophomoric rebellion. These days, Mom drinks water from a wineglass. I love that about her. She always ordered her Perrier "in a wineglass, please." Mom's got wicked style.

The rhythm to my parents' postdivorce relationship was staccato. They fought. If they weren't fighting, they were at best curt with each other. And if they weren't fighting, it was generally because I stirred up adolescent trouble. When there was a Jennifer issue, they joined forces and coalesced. It was obvious in the timbre of their voices on the telephone. I knew they were hearing each other in a new way, thankful for each other's parenting. They were in tune. It was sweet. What wasn't cool was being outside the loop. Being in trouble meant being out of the inner circle, even if they were "getting along." But for a moment, I could hear and somewhat feel them being together.

As far as dating goes, neither of my parents was big on the sport. Dad was always a family guy; it just took him a lot of figuring. Five wives. I've heard it said that jazz is just a note away from chaos. So, if missing the mark, one may be exquisitely close. It's amazing that Dad never lost faith in the institution of marriage. He was a relationship guy. He liked the day-to-days. I know he dated a bit when I was growing up, but seldom at best.

When Mom dated, I always knew and occasionally put up quite a stink. Poor Milos Forman. In that scathing adolescent way, I hated him. Mom and Milos dated for a while. One night they invited me to dinner. Mom was paying attention to her date. This guy, this hairy guy, was flirting with my mom right before my eyes. Who cares if he directed *One Flew Over the Cuckoo's Nest*? I threw a silent temper tantrum by lying down in the booth. Mom quickly escorted me to the car, where I spent the remainder of the meal. At least I didn't have to watch some flirty adult mess unfold.

Until about the age of twelve, nannies were a built-in piece of the household at Mom's and Dad's. Mom had a revolving door of "housekeeper, cook, nanny" women. Oddly, I don't remember any of them too well. They melded into one nanny figure who lived in a room just outside the house. Mom's work schedule was necessarily erratic. Someone had to "be there" for Jennifer. So, if Mom was off at an appointment, nanny woman was there. As far as I remember, Dad had a total of two nannies at 9966. Mom fired the first, Mimi, when she discovered Mimi's hidden gun. Literally. Mimi hid a gun in her purse. Not ideal for tending to an infant. So even when Mom wasn't

Willie joined us for our photo with the president. The Indian silk dress I wore was one of Dad's favorites. I believe this was taken in Century City, California, in 1974 or 1975.

there all the time, she kept watch, knew the score, and took care of business if need be. Thereafter, Dad hired the second, and only other, nanny, directly from Mom. Mom fired Willie and Dad hired her. Well, I liked Willie. So what if she wasn't a good housekeeper?

Willie Watson. "Don't you pay them no never mind. You pay attention to your business and let them take care of theirs. Easy as that." My best nanny of all time, by far. Pure, wise, simple, kind, and funny. Who could entertain a thought while catching a whiff of that mouthwatering-to-this-day chocolate cake? Willie had that Southern way of running the show without calling attention to the fact that she was running the show. Willie's eyes smiled when her mouth couldn't. Willie was no meek, take-orders type. Even when she seemed to comply, she did it her way in the end. After Barbara came to live with us, Willie had to go. Sadly, we lost our need for Willie. There just wasn't room enough for two women to run the show at 9966. Willie was the only "help" that managed to penetrate into the inner sanctum. Willie was, for many years, family.

Mom and Dad espoused polar opposite educational paradigms. A great deal of work went into choosing my grammar schools. True to form, Dad favored a highly disciplined, scholastically oriented program like that at Buckley, where I was made to curtsy and wear a proper uniform. Mom went with the more free-to-be, artistic, creative learning approaches such as Carden Malibu, where there were horses in the backyard and my jeans got dirty. Both of my parents were independent, driven, successful, talented, happy artists. Neither understood where my fondness for further education began. Mom regarded my algebra the way one might eyeball a new breed of animal—"What *is* that?"

Dad "homeschooled" me in life seven days a week. Though I attended kindergarten, grammar school, grade school, and the lot, Dad was there to daily supplement the curriculum. Essentially, he passed down a healthy curiosity for life and a love of learning. Dad educated through play. "How do you spell 'Nixon,' darling? N-I-X-

O-N. And who do you think our next president will be, darling?"
"Ford." "You know dear, I think you're right." I was well versed in
politics by the age of six.

WHEN IT CAME TIME for college, while excited about my commitment, Mom and Dad never mandated any prescribed course of
action. Their prerogative was my happiness. Dad's view was "If you
know what you want to do with your life, get out there and do it.
There's nothing that compares with on-the-job training. No school
like the school of hard knocks. Otherwise, college will buy you some
time, and there are some fascinating courses. . . . I wish I could
enroll." Dad was intrigued by formal education, but his route to
learning was life. Dad got kicked out of grade school for jumping
the fence to the girls' locker room. Mom served two years of college
before beelining to Los Angeles and acting. If I wanted a jump start,
it would come from my own passions, not pressure from home.
Mom and Dad both happily accepted my choice of Stanford. They
were proud of me for sticking with my education, wherever it might
lead. I liked the idea of law. . . . Mom thought it sounded neat, dramatic! She could see me on the courtroom floor, pleading someone's
case. Dad's dream scenario envisioned me as composer and mother.
Stay-at-home work. Funnily enough, neither parent wanted me to
act. It's the old do as I say, not as I do conundrum. Well, they were
both happy with their careers. So, challenging or not, eventually my
passions won out and drove me to acting, too.

Most of my childhood with Mom and Dad was spent as an only
child living with a single parent. It was either me and Mom or me
and Dad. Lots of intimate time. Lots of discussion. Lots of silence
and watching and really knowing another individual. It was difficult for anyone else to forge their way into that bond. So many years
of quiet togetherness, of staring one person in the face. . . . I had a
chance to know both of my parents in a unique way. No siblings
running around, vying for attention. Mom could fly me around on

her legs until I begged for release. "Nope," she'd say. "I'm going to send your dinner up there. Lamb chops in the air." No one else to push me from my pedestal. Dad and I could revel in "Pippy and Tippy" (our make believe birds) bedtime stories that were ours and ours alone. No third voice to chime in. Until the age of twelve, no

> SADLY, DEAR DAUGHTER OF MINE, I
> I MUST INFORM YOU THAT THIS BILL IS
> NOW YOUR RESPONSIBILITY — TO BE
> PAID, AS YOU MAY OBSERVE BY OCT 18th
> — BETTER STILL, IMMEDIATELY — AH, THE
> TASKS, THE VAGARIES OF LIFE —
> UNCEASING AND NECESSARY — THE
> BURDENS OF ADULTS — AND YOU ARE FAST !!!
> BECOMING ONE OF SUCH — BUT GREATLY loved..
>   Dad.

This note referenced either my phone bill or quarterly income taxes. By age twelve, I was given an account and directives to mail the necessary checks on time. Circa 1978.

major partners for either parent. Boyfriends and girlfriends, sure. But they were peripheral to our bond. We were the glue. I had plenty of friends, but my parents were my main buddies. They were my touchstones. I identified with Mom and Dad first. My formative experience of family is me and my parent. Two of us.

Chapter Fifteen

The Beautiful English Woman in Dad's Jennifer-Blue Cadillac

When I was about ten or so, Dad went to the Cadillac dealership to pick out a car and discovered the color Jennifer Blue. Now, as far as Cadillacs were concerned, Dad had a preference for white. Not this time. Dad drove a sky blue Cadillac for as many years as they made the color. He would excitedly announce to everyone within earshot, "It's Jennifer blue. It was listed next to all the other normal colors, pure white, crimson red, emerald green, and Jennifer blue!" Now here's a man who tailored his look. Style was in his bones. Simple. Classic. Less is more. And here he is driving a car that's *sky blue.* He enjoyed the meaning he derived from it.

When I met Barbara, she was sitting alongside Dad in the front seat of that same Jennifer-blue car. Barbara and Dad were waiting at the door of Mom's house at 98 Malibu Colony. It was Dad's weekend with me. I supposed since Barbara was in the front it meant I should sit in the back. Hmm. She seemed a little uptight. We had a two-hour drive to Palm Springs ahead of us . . . this could be bad. What I don't remember is Dad introducing the *idea* of Barbara. Presumably he alerted me to the fact that a new friend would be joining us for our weekend excursion to Uncle Charlie's. Did he say "friend"? "Girlfriend"? Hmm. Whatever the pretext, from the start, some-how, this one was different from his other "friends." For one, she was sitting in my seat. Unheard of.

Barbara recalls us hitting it off right away. She was quite ner-vous to meet me. I was the apple of her man's eye; it was important that things went smoothly between us. I was wary for different rea-sons. Dad was paying special attention to her. He watched after her the way he watched after me. That was annoying. She made him smile. Laugh even. Uh-oh. What could this mean? It's all over my face in some of the earliest photos of Barbara and me. I'm almost scowling. Sneering. As if to say, "Sure, I'll pose here and pretend we're best friends for you, Dad . . . yeah right." Something about the way he looked at her. There was admiration in it. Yeah, she was pretty, but that was icing. This woman had integrity, wit, style, ele-gance, all the social graces, and she was . . . sensible. Feminine, but no frills. Oh boy, this one would be challenging. I'd met only a cou-ple of other girlfriends and they didn't compare to this one at all.

I was used to getting all the attention, girlfriend or no. It was the first time I wanted to wear high heels in my life. I suppose I fix-ated on the heels as the defining difference between us. Barbara probably received attention because she wore adult sexy stuff. Attack the issue from the gross superficial level. At least it would minimize the differences. Well, I was twelve. Heels weren't an option. One inch max. I'd salivate at the sight of corkies in the shoe store window. The poor salesmen. I must've tried them on twenty or thirty times. I would strut around in a circle dreamily playing grown-up, attention-getting sexy woman for five minutes in the Malibu shoe store. Barbara's moving in with us was another first. Only two women had spent the night before this . . . but live with us? It was a graceful, natural transition. Now I could play sexy high heel lady in her closet, with her miraculous shoe collection—just don't let Dad catch us!

Dad met Barbara in London. She worked in public relations at the Royal Lancaster Hotel. Though he asked her to lunch immediately, it took Barbara quite a while to notice his attraction. The forty-six-year age gap threw her off the scent. Much to Dad's dismay she had a boyfriend, and when asked, she'd happily speak of him. Slowly but surely my father's persistence won her over.

The real pisser was that Barbara genuinely won me over. Even if she was a bit "English," proper and reserved. She was still fun. Silly fun. We'd create our own waltzes. Rascal fun. She'd fart in a public place and play it off as mine, aghast with "Jennifer!" Smart fun. She'd pander to the annoying tourists in our driveway. Barbara even told dirty jokes. With her ever so perfect accent, the foulest of language sounded docile. Damn.

Chapter Sixteen
Dad and Barbara

1970 · DAD'S BEDROOM AT 9966 BEVERLY GROVE DRIVE

Dad and I play make-believe. We're going to a party.

JG: Anni-re-versary party.
CG: Anni-re-versary? What's that?
JG: It means a wedding.
CG: Oh.
JG: It's a party in the snow. With bears.

Jennifer makes car sounds. We're driving to the party.

JG: Grrrrrrr . . . grrrrrrr . . . I'm the bear.

We play for a while. Go to many different parties . . .

CG: I'm tired of parties. I want to stay home and read a book.

Daisy, Daisy, give me your answer do . . . I'm half crazy all for the love of you. It won't be a stylish marriage. I can't afford a carriage. But you'd look sweet upon the seat of a bicycle built for two.

Okay, Dad wasn't big into bicycling anymore, and he could afford a carriage . . . but the tone still fits. Whatever physical magic they had, with Dad and Barbara it was friendship first. They were constantly together. When they met, Barbara was forging a promising career. My father cherished his time with Barbara and urged her to quit work. Eventually, happily for both of them, she succumbed. They had nine precious uninterrupted years together.

Prior to proposing marriage to Barbara, my father proposed his proposal to me. He literally asked my approval to marry. Dad flew up to Santa Catalina School for girls for a talk on the lawn. On a sunny, cool, crisp northern California afternoon we sat on the grass together and Dad let it all out. He needed to know my feelings. Would I be happy if they married? Would I resent her? Would I feel safe at home? Would I still know that he loved me and that nothing could ever come between us? Would I still want to visit? My room would always be my room. What did I think? Did I love her, too? Did I approve of his choice? My mother would always be my mother, but Barbara could be a good friend to me. Well. Shiver me timbers. Hell yes. "Yes, Dad. Marry her. Be happy together. I'm thrilled for you." "You know this will affect your inheritance, darling. You'll receive far less money if I marry Barbara. You'll split everything, but I'll give the house, which is worth quite a bit of money, to her." "Okay, Dad." What did the money mean to me at the time? Really. I'd always have plenty. Dad would be happy. They would be happy together. Their happy relationship benefited me, as well. When I was a child, my father's peace of mind was paramount to me. When the time came to venture off to college, knowing Barbara was by his side gave me the courage to spread my wings. I could leave the nest and know that he was well loved. Fly off on my own and know that someone would be there to make him smile and to care for him, every day and night, and I could at last relax. My dad was in love. Yes, Dad! Merrily marry Barbara!

My mother has often regarded Barbara in amazement—"I could never be that." Mom and Barbara are two such different women. Mom is a "doer" of the first order. A career woman. Barbara loves being married, caring for the nest, the garden, her friends, and her man and not necessarily working. It's who they are. However different they may be, they share the *Steel Magnolia* quality. Two beautiful, in their own ways feminine, and powerfully strong women. I lucked out.

In those awful, the-world-is-an-ugly-place moments, when I'm busy mistaking my darkness for depth, my thoughts have visited the dark side with Barbara. Here's a piece of that monologue: "He was old. She was young, beautiful, active, strong. Why not be with a young man? Why be stuck in the house with an eighty-something-year-old dude? Even if he was Cary Grant. Did she want fame? She didn't have to put up with him for long, and then she was financially set for life. Money grubber!" Well. Here's the rub. I saw her love *him.* Not Cary Grant the legend, but Cary Grant the sometimes quite difficult to live with man. Barbara "got" him. She shared his precise nature, his attention to detail, and empathized with the man whose scrupulous conscience kept him awake at night. She could actually explain his anxieties to me in ways I'd never before imagined. I watched her lose twenty pounds when he died. We shared the loss of his love and I could feel it on her. And then . . . we helped each other step out of our black holes, as we continue to now. If Dad were a five-foot-tall, middle-class, eighty-year-old from Poughkeepsie, he wouldn't have been Cary Grant—the man we happened to love. Look, who wouldn't want the money—right? Perhaps in typical only-child fashion I should've inherited everything! My sincere bet is if Barbara could've had him for twenty more years, she'd have gladly pushed for twenty-five. All the flowers, the cards, the hollow flash of fame, the taffeta, the silk and diamonds, the real estate, the prominent connections — terrific stuff as it is, in the face of losing one's partner . . . it's a hill o' beans.

Faith in my family, which includes Barbara, takes far more courageous introspection than bowing to the skepticism of vilification. Vilification, which at its root is bleak, undigested self-flagellation. "Barbara must have had ulterior motives" is cagily disguised "I would have been better by his side" thinking, flagellation of the "why didn't I do more for him? Why wasn't I always there to meet his every need?" egotistic sort. If I accept that it was okay to go off to school and become a "young woman" leading her own life, then I accept that it was okay for Barbara and Dad to have their life without me. I wasn't needed the way I used to be. That's okay. I didn't leave him at home with a monster, I left him at home with someone who loved him and cared for him in ways I never could or should have. Prior to their marriage, I was closest to Dad. After their marriage, we all shared that bond. For the last several years of his life, Dad needed his companion, mate, friend, lover, and partner at his side. Dad needed his Barbara.

BARBARA AND DAD went the uncommon extra mile for each other. In 1981 Barbara had the excellent good sense to assemble a birthday tape for Dad with messages from pals around the globe. Barbara sent cassette tapes with instructions for each participant to record their own personalized birthday message for Dad. Barbara then compiled these tapes into one grand birthday tape. The endeavor began as a one-time thing, but it was such a tremendous hit that Barbara served it up a second year. Actually, I think a couple of the tapes missed their deadline, providing Barbara the impetus for a follow-up. The roster was impressive.

Jennifer	Jennifer
Charlie Rich	George Burns
Fred de Cordova	Bobby Altman
Johnny Carson	George Steinbrenner
Glenn & Cynthia Ford	Cy Coleman
Roddy Mann	Walter Cronkite
Frank & Barbara Sinatra	Irene Selznick
Norton & Jennifer Simon	Cubby & Dana Broccoli
Gregory & Veronique Peck	Jimmy Stewart
Princess Grace	Danny Kaye
Irving Lazar	Peter O'Malley
Stanley Fox Family	Dan Melnick
Maggie & Eric Leach	Stanley Donen
Barbara	Peter Bogdanovich
	Sammy Cahn
	Katharine Hepburn
	Tom Lasorda
	President & Betty Ford
	President & Nancy Reagan
	Barbara

These loving birthday messages played like some fabulous personalized combination of Kennedy Center Honors and Friars Club
roast. Princess Grace read "The Owl and the Pussycat" in melt-
you-to-the-core perfect pitch. Sammy Cahn doodled tailor-made for
Cary versions of songs on his piano. "The Most Beautiful Girl in the
World" became "The Most Wonderful Man in the World," and "A
Touch of Class" had added Grant pizzazz. Johnny Carson's message to Dad: "You're just terrific and I would've liked to have been
with you on this occasion, but it's my bowling night. I'm with the
alpha beta bombers, I know you'll understand. . . ." Frank Sinatra
crooned, "Happy birthday to you, happy birthday to you, happy
birthday dear Cary, happy birthday to you. . . . That'll be five thou-

Their love was evident. It just felt good to be around them. On the patio of 9966, 1981.

sand dollars." Tommy Lasorda's greeting: "Hi Cary . . . you know I've just found out that you were an acrobat before you went into the movies. I've been thinking what an outstanding shortstop you would have made. . . . Just think how many pennants you could've helped the Dodgers win by now." Stanley Donen, who directed Dad in *Charade,* styled his own poem:

> *There once was an actor named Grant.*
> *He gave life a happier slant.*
> *His talents fantastic*
> *On-screen and gymnastic,*
> *But he never learned how to say "can't."*
> *His acting was all double duty.*
> *He deserved all the fame and the booty.*
> *No one else in our crowd*
> *Will be ever allowed*
> *To say*
> *Judy Judy Judy Judy Judy.*
> *I've known him as actor and friend.*
> *Our conflicts always had an end.*
> *When we'd disagree*

On script or on fee
He was rigid so I had to bend.
The problems he posed me were vast
I want Bergman, I want Hepburn, make it fast!
Then I'd fly off to Rome
Or Paris, alone
And they'd do it with him in the cast.
He's known as the ultimate in tact.
For elegance there's nothing he lacked.
But the hours of pleasure
That I'll always treasure
Are in a theater watching Cary Grant act.
So tonight is a birthday for Cary.
Shoot rockets, fire cannon, be merry
You can search, you can seek
He's truly unique
Do we love him, oh yes we do . . . very.
Happy Birthday Cary.

Ingrid Bergman shared her love, too: "Dear birthday child. This is a message to wish you a very happy birthday. I'm a little embarrassed because I've never given birthday wishes over a tape recorder. I think it's a very nice idea except I'm a little stuck for words. But I'll tell you I remember a long time ago when you and I were working on a picture, and I came over one morning full of excitement and said to you, 'You know that together you and I are one hundred years old?' And you didn't like that joke very much. So, I'm not going to repeat it. . . . I'm not going to even think about how old together we would be today. Not having a personal script writer I think I'll read something that was sent to me long ago; I have no idea who it was who wrote it, but it is a prayer and it's something that you must've read earlier because it's very much what you have done. The kind of life you have had. But I'll read it to you anyway—it goes . . .

Give me a good digestion, Lord, and also something to digest.
Give me a healthy body, Lord, with sense to keep it at its best.

Give me a healthy mind, Lord, to keep the good and pure in sight,
which, seeing sin, is not appalled, but finds a way to set it right.
Give me a mind that is not bored, that does not whimper, whine or sigh.
Don't let me worry much about the fussy thing called I.
Give me a sense of humor, Lord. Give me the grace to see a joke.
To get some happiness from life, and pass it on to other folk.

"Well . . . that's it. And you see what I mean, Cary. You have lived accordingly. That's why you have many friends and we're very happy to think about you, remember the good old days, and today especially, send you the best wishes for the future, for all your heart desires. From your old friend—and here's the same joke: You're *Notorious* and *Indiscreet* and as Hitch would say, 'the old bat', Ingrid."

President Gerald Ford and his wife, Betty, sent a joint message that included a story of inauguration night:

> President Ford: "Hi Cary, this is Gerry Ford wishing you a very, very happy birthday."
> Betty Ford: "And Betty Ford here too wishing you the very same."
> President Ford: "We're there in spirit if not in person. As you well know we've admired you so many years. We cherish, we treasure your friendship."
> Betty Ford: "Cary, you have no idea how many tapes it has taken to get this far. We're just not the pros that you are. But we know you understand. I think often of that very celebrated night when I had the opportunity of having you as an escort for a very special occasion and I remember well how all the rest of the girls said when they saw the picture of us dancing together, 'Wow! What a man!' Well, we all still feel that way and this is your special day. . . . All the best."
> President Ford: "I second everything Betty has said and there's no way we can adequately express our gratitude for your friendship and to wish you the happiest possible birthday."

President and Nancy Reagan improvised their birthday greeting:

President Reagan [to Nancy, hushed, aside]: "Is this a dinner or something they're giving?"

Nancy Reagan: "No dear, it's her . . . well, she might have a dinner for him, but it's her surprise present for Cary. And she did this for him once before and he was very touched. Some people told funny stories that concerned him and some people just talked about what a nice man he is. . . ."

President Reagan: "All right . . . [Then, louder, to microphone] Well, Nancy . . ."

Nancy Reagan: "Well, don't say Nancy."

President Reagan: "Why?"

Nancy Reagan: "Because you're talking to Cary."

President Reagan: "Yes, but I thought we were doing it as a dialogue."

Nancy Reagan: "No dear."

President Reagan: "Oh, we each say something separate. . . . Forgive me, Cary, my wife won't talk to me, so I'll talk to you. [Nancy laughs] . . . Cary, now that we're straightened away here, I suppose the first thing to say is happy birthday. And for whatever help it might be to you, for a long time now I haven't been having them myself. I've just been having anniversaries of my thirty-ninth birthday. But it is a pleasure to have been invited to participate even in this remote way and to be able to not only congratulate you on your birthday, but tell you how much your friendship has meant and how very much we wish we could be there with you, so God bless you."

Nancy Reagan: "Cary, I'm going to tell you a story that I'm sure you've probably forgotten, but— As a very scared, nervous newcomer to the picture business and Metro, I'll never forget how you were to me when I was trying out for a picture with you. I've forgotten the name of the picture. But I remember you were the star and I wanted very much to play opposite you. I didn't get the part and it just broke my heart and you of course knew that and you took me to lunch and you were so dear, and so sweet, and so nice, as you always are. But I've never forgotten it, and I really wish I could be there in person and wish you a happy birthday and give you a big kiss and a hug for being so nice to that young girl."

ESTABLISH GUIDE LINES, BUT GIVE FREEDOM WITHIN THOSE LINES.

MY PERSONAL BELIEF IS THAT IT'S THE GOOD THAT WE DO FOR THE LIVING THAT COUNTS. WHATEVER WE DO FOR THE DEAD IS REALLY DONE FOR OURSELVES.

CONGRATULATIONS ON PASSING THE TEST FOR YOUR OPERATORS LICENSE. YOUR CAR KEYS WERE GIVEN TO YOU WITH THE UNDERSTANDING THAT YOU WILL BEHAVE AS A RESPONSIBLE YOUNG ADULT. YOUR KEYS, LIKE YOUR OPERATOR'S LICENSE, ARE PROBATIONARY--YOURS SO LONG AS THEY ARE USED WITH COMMON SENSE AND COURTESY BUT THEY WILL BE TAKEN FROM YOU IF YOU HAVE ABUSED THE PRIVILEGE. WE REALIZE ANYONE CAN HAVE AN ACCIDENT BUT PLEASE DRIVE DEFENSIVELY AT ALL TIMES. YOUR MOTHER AND I ARE WILLING TO PAY FOR THE EXTRA INSURANCE AND GASOLINE SO LONG AS THE ABOVE CONDITIONS ARE FOLLOWED. WE ASK ONLY THAT YOU LET US KNOW WHERE YOU ARE GOING AND WHO WILL BE RIDING WITH YOU.

MARRIAGE:
IT'S VERY BEAUTIFUL AND FINE AND VERY DIFFICULT. IT'S BEING HAPPY AND SHARING IT WITH SOMEBODY AND BEING ANGRY AND SHARING THAT TOO. IT'S A KINDNESS, A GENTLENESS, LAUGHTER, THAT FLOWS BETWEEN PEOPLE. IT'S HAVING SOMEONE THERE WHEN YOU'RE ILL. IT'S LIKE A LIGHT LEFT ON IN THE HALL WHEN YOU GO TO BED. IT'S A SORT OF BLESSING: ROBERT NATHAN

THE ABOVE FOR MY BELOVED WIFE.

Dad compiled such quotes for Barbara and me along with several pages of guidelines from the "Love Is . . ." comic strip.

President Reagan: "So shall we both say happy birthday now again? . . . and Cary, this is the first time I've heard that story and I'm going to continue the dialogue with Nancy after we get off these microphones. . . ."
Both: "Happy Birthday Cary!"

Barbara produced the sweetest star-studded tribute of all time. She loved Dad, loved seeing him happy, and knew how to make it happen. In choosing my father as her partner, Barbara knowingly put aside her desire to have children. Dad was seventy-seven when they wed. His child was mostly grown. It was Dad's gentle hour, to be spent with his companion, friend, and mate, Barbara. But what of Barbara's life after Dad? Almost certainly they both knew he'd leave the world before she did, and she might never again have a chance to reproduce. Yes, Barbara and I were and are close, but having a child of your own is one of life's dearest treasures. Barbara would have been a genius at mothering, and she knowingly gave that up. Dad didn't want her to make that sacrifice. Beginning at age eighty, Dad tried to give Barbara a child. When it didn't work as they had hoped, Dad asked if Barbara would consider being inseminated with a donor's sperm. The year of his death, they were on that road. At twenty- or thirty-something, it's hard enough to wake through the night, change diapers, rock a crying baby to sleep, and turn your world upside down with an infant's needs. So imagine the selflessness of this act for an eighty-two-year-old Cary Grant who was accustomed to being the star in his well-earned, perfectly contained oasis. Perhaps Barbara and Dad both sensed his time was running short. Perhaps a new child would hold Dad to this earth. Or, perhaps if he did have to go, at least his wife would have the comfort of new life at her side. Sadly, they never made that new life. We all have our trade-offs.

Auntie Sylvia believes Dad pursued Barbara because he spotted a strong ally in her. If it's tough to face life alone, death's approach likely made it that much tougher for Dad, as well. Barbara could be his travel mate for the final journey. Perhaps a loved one's eyes can cushion the blow to the hereafter. Barbara could be an ally for his daughter, too. Well, if so, Dad was correct. The term "stepmother," not unlike the term "mother-in-law," gets, in general, a bad rap. Not in my case.

I use the French term *belle mere,* which literally translates as "beautiful mother," to refer to Barbara. We have often gratefully acknowledged our relationship. We didn't have to be friends. I've seen many families torn apart by the reading of the will. Money can get ugly. We have the classic "trappings" that could easily have driven us to ruin. Still, together with my father, we constructed a family that we "carry" forward through the years.

The main reason Dad and Barbara worked so perfectly is that they wanted the same things in life. They put intimacy, coupledom, and relationship above all else. Dad was the masculine thinker, planner, and "doer," and Barbara the feminine, receptive, intuitive "feeler." Of course, she was masterful at gently bending things her way. If Barbara ran the show from backstage, no one else knew it. Especially Dad. Barbara knows the art of gently planting a seed that later takes root as someone else's idea. "Darling, I just had a thought . . ." *Oh really? . . .* Successful couples are like Rubik's Cubes to me. . . . How do they do it? In Barbara and Dad's case, they made it look easy. I suppose ultimately it is. Dad wanted to eat English cucumber sandwiches, and Barbara delighted in cutting off the crusts for him. They shared the same values, they agreed on mutually complementary roles, and they honored these values by living them.

Chapter Seventeen
The Grants

The Grants" refers to Dad, Barbara, and myself. Since my parents split when I was but a babe, though I may have some unconscious knowing of their togetherness, I don't really remember us being a family. The Grants was my first nuclear family experience. Our family rhythm was light, silly fun. We referred to ourselves as the Grunts: Poppa Grunt, Missus Grunt, and Baby Grunt. Some families bicker constantly, stage big dramatic fights, pontificate, or find their union in spirited debate. It's a dance. It seems we establish certain steps and a tempo sparks. A chemical reaction. At times I still feel like a child around my family. My feet begin doing their habitual two-step before a syllable is uttered.

The Grunts generally combusted into play. Play was a cornerstone in our lives. We were dynamic goofballs. One of Dad's favorite tongue twisters was "Black bug's blood." Say it ten times as quickly as you can. Because Dad was in his seventies and eighties in my teen years, game play was generally of the tame, mind-bent variety. We weren't the snowboarding, touch-football-playing, rock-climbing, Rollerblading types. We went the way of card games, board games, guesstimating distance games, hangman, word scrambles, memory games, magic tricks, television game shows, and the ever popular "roll around in a ball in the backseat while Dad swerved the Cadillac like a madman" game. Remember the nonsensical singsongy rhyme in *The Bachelor and the Bobby-Soxer?*

A: "You remind me of a man."
B: "What man?"
A: "The man with the power."
B: "What power?"
A: "The power of voodoo."
B: "Who do?"
A: "You do."
B: "Do what?"
A: "Remind me of a man . . ."

Under the Golden Gate Bridge on one of our Princess Alaskan cruises, circa 1980. With my own room, and therefore my own key, I felt all grown-up on these trips.

And so on ad infinitum. At least once a week, for as many years as I can remember, one or the other of us would randomly begin our ritualistic nonsensical prayer. From down the hall I'd hear, "Hey . . . by the way . . . you remind me of a man . . ." Nothing to say, but wanting to engage in blithe togetherness. "Oy . . . have I told you lately? You remind me of a man . . ."

NOVEMBER 21, 1970 · DAD'S BEDROOM AT 9966

Dad sings to me.

CG: "Oh horsey keep your tail up, keep your tail up, keep your tail up, oh horsey keep your tail up, keep the sun out of my eyes."

Dad and I place stuffed animals on an improvised "tissue paper" hammock, which occasionally breaks as we swing my various dolls.

CG: Daddy's tired. He's been traveling for quite a while to London for a charity for Prince Philip and his wildlife foundation. Dad sat on the right of Queen Juliana.

Their wedding day. Barbara would have loved to invite her family, but for reasons known only to him, Dad insisted on it being just the three of us. On the patio of 9966, 1981.

No response from Jennifer.

CG: I was doing a lot of name dropping. Didn't you hear me?

Dad speaks to the tape recorder as Jennifer gives dolls rides on the swing.

CG: Jennifer's bed faces mine so that when we awaken we can see each other across the length of the room.
JG: I'm going to be five.
CG: Time flies. I want it to go slower.

Jennifer goes over to Daddy's "magic drawer."

JG: Let's see if the magic drawer has something for us? . . . Not yet.
CG: Sometimes when she opens it, there's something that Jennifer has never seen before. It's magic.

Daddy and Jennifer tie laces on "tidy lace-up" doll.

CG: Daddy's tired because it's two forty-five a.m. in London and here it's just past teatime.

{Then singing} "Please put a penny in the old man's hat."

JG [singing]: "Christmas is coming the goose is getting fat. Please put a penny in the old man's hat. If you haven't got a penny a ha'penny will do . . ."
CG: Darling, it's pronounced "hay-penny."
JG [singing]: "If you have no hay-penny then God bless you."
CG: "Merrily we roll along, roll along, roll along . . ."
JG: "Mary had a little lamb, little lamb, little lamb . . ."
CG: You know, those sound alike. Oh no! You're going to swing teddy bear and hit Julie and George.
JG: Don't tell them!

Daddy laughs.

JG: We won't be your best friends.
CG: I want you to be my best friend.
JG: I will if you stop kicking me.

Dad cracks up.

CG: This is being taped!

Later . . .

CG: Darling, you have two of those books, please give one to
    Willie, for her grandsons.
JG: I made something for you in Mrs. Knowles's class.

Jennifer Scotch tapes a new drawing on Daddy's wall.

CG: You are very generous.
JG: The drawer is magic, but you put everything in it.
CG: How do you know?
JG: I know.
CG: How do you know it wasn't the good fairy?
JG: I don't have one yet cuz I didn't lose a tooth.
CG: You get a fairy when you lose a tooth?
JG: Yes, but you get money, not candy.

Chapter Eighteen

It's Okay to Be a Pip

As Dad used the word, a "pip" is something full of mischief, a nuisance, or a general inconvenience, be it a person, place, or thing. A flat tire might be a pip. An acoustically challenged restaurant, where it's difficult to be heard without raising your voice, was a pip. The Grants were definite pips.

Maybe being a pip was part of my father's winsome charm, on-screen or off. Pips have that little twinkle in their eye, which indicates something fun could happen at any moment. Take Dad and Katharine Hepburn in *Bringing Up Baby*. Dad and Katharine Hepburn in anything. They liked to outpip each other.

When asking Dad to reconsider my curfew, or to bend the rules and get a dog, I was a pip. Dad was totally against having animals at home. Dogs and cats were "unsanitary." He said they brought a multitude of germs into the house. I was allowed to have fish and turtles. I was never that crazy about the fish, but I *loved* the turtles. I liked the feel of their little scratchy claws on my hand. We kept them in the pantry. Odd place for turtles, now that I think about it. Of course, our pantry was the size of my current kitchen, so it's not as though the turtles were crammed in next to the condiments. I could sit there, play with my turtles, and watch Willie prepare lunch or dinner. Every few years I placed a new request for a puppy or a kitten. Denied!

Lucky for me, Barbara was a coconspiratorial pip. It took her quite a while, but slowly she worked away at Dad, softening his resolve about pets. Her pip was patient. After they had been together several years Barbara got a cat. Hooray! EQ, short for the musical term "equalize" was a white cat with one blue eye and one green eye. Hence the equalize/equal-eyes pun. Since EQ went over well enough, shortly thereafter Barbara miraculously summoned her a friend named Sausage. One fine day a beautiful dark cat appeared at the front door. Barbara undoubtedly performed her best bewitching spells because Dad allowed the cat *inside* the house. Even more astonishing, Dad fell head over heels for Sausage.

Of course, just then, in a Murphy's law sort of way, the cat's proper owner materialized. Barbara arranged a time for the owner to retrieve Sausage. However, at the arranged pickup, the ungrateful man sent envoys in his stead. Dad reasoned that if the man couldn't be bothered to fetch his feline friend, fat chance he'd find him. Dad hid Sausage in the washroom. "Oops . . . he must've trotted off somewhere." Pip. Finally they arranged a direct handoff. New tactics required. Dad was smitten. . . . He didn't want to let go of sweet Sausage. Poppa and Missus Grunt outlined a plan. They would pay the sad, lowly bugger off. The man arrived in a Rolls and Dad's heart sank. Negotiations began. The resulting deal was a truly Los Angeles agreement. Shared custody of Sausage. Lucky for Dad, a few weeks later the former owner gave up his rights entirely.

I was in boarding school in northern California at the time, but whenever Dad and I spoke, much to my amazement, he never failed to mention Sausage's progress. My father was absolutely transfixed by this cat. Sausage was a dark gray boy, with little white patches on his chest and front paw. I think he reminded Dad of himself, particularly in his youth; lithe, sleek, fun, and focused. Dad went from a staunch feline opponent to a cat lover, all because of Sausage. He spoke of his new friend with obvious delight: "He's simply marvelous. You should see the way he jumps, and then waits, casually, silently, calculating his next move, until all at once he's up and pouncing on some new target."

One sad day I called home and Barbara warned me that something terrible had happened. Sausage had gotten out of the house and been eaten by a coyote. Poor Dad was miserable. He relived it for months. He'd grown painfully close to the cat and could hardly bear it. It gave me some understanding of his begrudging us animals in the first place. Sure, he cited the germs, and eventually gave in "for Barbara," but once the cats were inside the house, he surrendered completely. Perhaps he knew his heart was at their mercy. I'd never seen him so sad as when Sausage died. Still, Dad agreed that Sausage was worth the heartache. Thereafter we always had cats.

Barbara generally played the pip to make us happy and give us a giggle. Though brilliant come game time, Dad was painfully nervous prior to speaking engagements. The nerves must have driven his performance because he was consistently magnificent and always overprepared for a speech. The downside was that 9966 was uptight for a day or two before, as Dad crafted his thoughts and carefully copied key lines for his note cards. Note cards that most often stayed in his pockets. The night of one somewhat tedious affair, Dad was introducing so-and-so at a very stuffy sit-down dinner. The still mingling meeting and greeting audience was obviously humorless. Well, Barbara would occasionally sidle up behind my father during the cocktail hour and, underneath his jacket, unbeknownst to all, "goose" him by quietly giving his privates a little squeeze. Dad would then turn, slyly smiling, and introduce his genteel wife. Well, this particular evening, while facing me, Barbara did her best, subtlest goose and received no response. My face went pale. She had goosed the wrong tall gray-haired gentleman. "So sorry!" Barbara immediately trotted off and made apologies to the man's wife. Pip, indeed.

Dad once outed me in fine pip fashion. Throughout my childhood I enjoyed various forms of dance. Baryshnikov was my near idol because of his particular blend of grace and boyish charm. Luckily for me, on the evening that the Kennedy Center honored my father, Baryshnikov danced. After the performance, Dad introduced me to the marvelous Russian dancer: "This is my daughter, Jennifer. She's quite enamored with you." I turned twenty shades of pink. Enamored? I'm thirteen! He's hot! Now I look like a total doof. DAD! Pip.

I liked to swipe Dad's money. My father kept his cash in a bathroom drawer. I was quite familiar with Dad's "money drawer" because I had a fascination with counting his money. It was all lined up in the same direction, smaller denominations to the outside. Once in a while I would steal from his gold clip. A five here, a ten or maybe even a twenty there . . . never anything that was detected. Or was it? I always wondered if he knew. Perhaps I was in utter disbelief that anything crept past his scrutiny. Perhaps Dad kept the closest watch on himself and allowed the rest of us a bit more room for trespass. Of course, I was given an allowance, so I never really needed the money. Pip girl just wanted to see if she could get away with it. Sometimes what Dad loved best about me was my "pip" . . . the part of me that messed up, that wanted what I wanted because I wanted it. Maybe his Capricorn goat Bristol boy could relate. Catching me filching a precious chocolate from his drawer, he'd smile a sideways loopy grin. "Dear, dear Jennifer." My antics tickled him.

We had a "You should see the view" view. Stunning. From downtown Los Angeles all the way to the beach—oh, but please don't. All my life we had looky loos parking outside the gate and peering in through the metal bars. Our home was on the Movie Star Maps. Can't blame people for wanting to see, really, but it was a disconcerting inconvenience. People would park their cars in our driveway, just outside the gate. Then they'd stand and gaze in and around the gate, hoping to catch a glimpse of Dad through the windows or in the backyard. Dad, Barbara, and I likened it to being animals in a zoo.

One Sunday, when a family remained parked and leering for a particularly long period of time, using the intercom box alongside the gate Barbara asked, "Would you like some peanuts?" The tonal quality was akin to "Who the f—— do you think you are?" They startled, looking about for the voice's source. Finally one bright soul figured it out. Not sure they delighted in our joke, but we wore Cheshire cat grins. One of my favorite pictures of Dad, Barbara, and me is a spoof on all of this. In the midst of a rarely held family photo session (perhaps our only one), we decided to get a shot of us at the gate, mimicking our imagined status as displeased monkeys, our cheeks puffed and heads pressed through the bars. Of course, we did choose the outside of the gate as the imagined cage. We quite liked our own confines.

Our most problematic visitor used to lay himself across our driveway, forbidding our entrance or exit. Our entry toll was listening to his repeated sermon. According to him, Dad was his father by Queen Elizabeth. This man had been cheated of both his title and his fortune and he was outraged. He would block our driveway until we heeded his rambling homily, then we could freely pass. Must say, he didn't look a bit like Dad or Queen Elizabeth. Though I was never there to witness it, a few times the police had to be summoned to physically remove him. Pre–Movie Star Maps we used the driveway and a patch of grass at the side of the house at playtime. I learned to ride a tricycle there. From ages three to six, I used the driveway to play catch with Dad and my favorite large, yellow, spotted plastic ball. Badminton took place on the grass during the summers. Post–Movie Star Maps, all activities moved into the front yard, where we were shielded from our own street. . . . Sometimes life's a pip. An avid fan might imagine Grace Kelly, Dad, Hitch, and

*Monkeys at the 9966
gates, circa 1983.*

a group of pals cavorting on the lawn in linens with Pimm's
Cups . . . perhaps a stray shuttlecock would float over the fence and
said fan could retrieve it and be invited in for the badminton game.
No. Ninety-five percent of the time behind the gates meant family
time.

Chapter Nineteen
Dad and Me: Slow Like Stew

A broad margin of leisure is as beautiful in a man's life as in a
book. Haste makes waste, no less in life than in housekeeping.
Keep the time, observe the hours of the universe, not of the
railroad cars. What are three score years and ten hurriedly and
coarsely lived, to moments of divine leisure in which your life
is coincident with the life of the universe? We live too fast and
coarsely, just as we eat food too fast, and do not know the true
savor of our food.

—*Thoreau*

7:30 A.M. NOVEMBER 28, 1970

*Daddy and Jennifer sing songs together over the telephone. We start with
"The Hokey Pokey." Daddy continues singing after I've stopped.*

JG: Tomorrow since you're a silly Daddy I won't have you on the
telephone anymore.

CG: Oh no! Please. I won't be funny anymore. [Then] I don't
deny it, I will be quiet.
JG [sings]: "John Jacob Jingleheimer Schmidt, his name is my
name too, whenever we go out the people always shout, John
Jacob Jingleheimer Schmidt."
CG [singing along]: "Da da da da da da dum . . ."

A few moments later . . .

CG: Happy Thanksgiving, my darling, my beloved. Jennifer, I
wanted to tell you that the other night, in England, I met a
man. The first man to walk on the moon . . .

From the start, reliable as daybreak, Dad was there for me. He
bared his all in love and held nothing back. From the day-to-day
detail to life's blockbuster moments, my father was there. This
didn't mean he was always pleased with me, but happy or not, if he
could help it, he wasn't ever going away.

The Fabergé jet was at Dad's disposal to visit wherever in the
world I might be. Dad loved his job as a director and had a close
friend in George Barrie, Fabergé's president. If I was on school holiday, there was always the remote possibility of Mom bringing me to
a movie set in some distant location. Dad wanted to be sure that he
could get to me. Dad wanted me to know that men could be trusted
to fulfill their promises. Though the location was never too terribly
remote, Dad did bring the plane to fetch me in Paris while Mom
was shooting *The Last of Sheila.* Of course, at age six, I had no idea to
what lengths he'd gone to see me. I just knew that it was my time to
be with Daddy, *et bien sûr,* he'd be there. Even when it wasn't "his"
time he made his presence felt. One of Auntie Sylvia's favorite
remembrances is Dad parking his car at a stop along my grade
school bus route. That way we could have a glimpse of each other
each morning. If only for an instant, we could see each other
through the bus window and wave.

My father's love left reminders. When he went away, he sent
thoughtful, cleverly worded postcards. At Christmas, each gift had

a playful note attached. If he gave me a stock or a bond the note might read: "You're sure to find interest in this . . ." For a book on horses, "Canter-very tales?" We said the words, too. Our family was big on "I love you." Morning, afternoon, and evening. Dad wasn't afraid to say it. In person, on the phone, in front of school, at the stables, alone, in front of others, first thing in the morning, and last thing at night. When heartfelt, those three words hold their meaning regardless of repetition.

Dad and I liked to pal around together. We were chums. Dad's seventies Colony house was just a few doors down from Mom's. Both homes were on the beach side of the street. A two-minute walk from one to the other. That way when it wasn't his time with me he could watch me at play on the beach. Dad often filmed passersby from his deck. Kids taunting the waves, horses trotting along the sand, lovers walking hand in hand, and skim boarders falling on their bums. In one of his home movies Mom and I briefly walk by at a distance. Doubtful anyone besides a trained expert would catch it, I'm surprised I did . . . but seeing the Super 8 gave me a sense of his loneliness. His longing. Some years later, his Colony house then a memory, he staged a Colony surprise for me. It was Halloween and I was about twelve. All the kids were out, running from house to house, doing their candy collecting, "egging," and the rest. Word trickled down early that Dad was in the "big house." The wooden barnlike one with the huge anchor thing on the front. Dad rented it *for one night* to surprise me. This is one of those if-only-I-could-take-it-back moments. I was embarrassed that he was there. Embarrassed that he would go to such lengths for me. I felt I was being hyperwatched. In a way, it was true. I ran up to the door and tried to pretend like it was just another house. Just a guy giving out candy. I took it and ran. If only . . . I'd drop my stupid pumpkin and jump into his bearlike arms right now.

There were no cell phones then, and alone time had a different flavor. The technology of the day suited our family. We were the slow-cooking types. Like stew. Nothing instant about us. No TV dinners, microwaves, or e-mailing on a BlackBerry at a stoplight. Things took time. We had conversations. It was quieter in those days, fewer intrusions. Dad listened to me. He didn't just take me along for the ride. Dad had the luxury of choosing retirement. Still, he was a prominent public figure and remained active in the business world. So Dad made me a part of that business world. If he had a meeting coming up, he discussed it with me. "Isn't it amazing . . . Kirk's planning on building this great new hotel in Vegas." When he had board meetings, he made sure I had plans, too. I wasn't shuttled along in the car and made to wait.

In the larger scheme, Dad wanted me to have the sense of doing things for myself, without unnecessary loneliness. He was an only child, too. There are times when life seems quiet from that perspective. Generally I attended tennis or riding lessons on my own. One out of ten times, Dad stayed to see my progress on the horse or the court. When he was there, he'd heartily encourage my strengths and laugh at my foibles. I loved it.

Dad let me take risks. Physical risks. At seventy-something, he confidently watched me be my best tomboy self and earn my gaming stripes. He knew he could pick me up if and when I fell. Dad photographed Lisa and me, age ten, tandem jumping from the rope swing at Carden Malibu School. The two tenacious girls high atop a platform full of boys. Looks *fun*! Supported by a huge eucalyptus branch, we slip our feet side by side into a rope noose and merrily swing out over the expanse of playground. Still gives me a chill. How did Dad stomach it?

Dad's trust encouraged my gently blithe sense of adventure. One fine afternoon in the archives I came upon pictures of me, eyes closed, practicing balance moves on the two-inch lip of the living-room couch. Dad videotaped it. But who is this entirely unflappable nonchalant creature blindly performing balance maneuvers, on one foot, atop a skinny homemade balance beam? How many

July 20, 1969

Today, Sunday, July 20th, 1969 man landed on the moon. The
Lunar module... "Eagle"...touched down on the moon's surface at
4:17 p.m., Eastern Time, here in Miami where I am...and where
I miss you...and at 1:17 p.m., in Beverly Hills where you are.
Some four hours later Commander Neil Armstrong took man's first
step onto the moon's surface. He was followed by Astronaut Colonel
Edwin Aldrin, Jr. The attached brochure brought from the Florida
launching site of Apollo Eleven, the missile which blasted them out
into Space, explains how their historic mission was accomplished.

By the time you are grown up, such space journeys may be
commonplace and even the longer journey to Mars, which seems
more able to support the continuance of life as we humanbeings
know it, might be taking place. However, to date, it is man's
greatest achievement in Space.

It is late Sunday night as I write so, unfortunately, your envelope
cannot be stamped with the actual date of the landing on the moon;
where both Astronauts now rest inside the Lunar module prior to an
attempt to project their vehicle back into space and rejoin Astronaut
Lieutenant-Colonel Michael Collins who orbits in the mother space-
ship that hopefully will carry them back to our Earth.

Yesterday, and today, the people of our Nation, and throughout
the entire world, are united in prayer for the safe-being of these three
brave Americans.

You are always in my thoughts, Jennifer, and my dearest wish is
to live long enough to read and study the enclosed brochures with you
...perhaps on our way to Mars.

I love you.

Perhaps I can still meet him there?

times had he watched me fall? What was I thinking? Quite simply, I knew he'd be there, and, even more important, I could feel the confidence he had in me.

Dad taped me in the process of learning to ride a bicycle. Goodbye to the training wheels. Up and down the Colony I go. It's a hoot to watch me starting and stopping, floundering around, unable to figure out a balanced start-up. My friend Rachel Culp dutifully runs alongside to get me going. Time and again my bike goes zigzagging down the street, eventually veering to a stop just short of hitting some nearby car or garage door. But just a video minute later the tape goes on to show me successfully balancing and merrily riding off into the distance. Hell, I could even turn! Today, riding my bike home from yoga class, something dawned on me. Perhaps the things I envision for myself but still haven't mastered are like riding that bike. Expect wobbles at first (laugh if possible). But perhaps one day, I'll merrily ride off into the distance. So simple. The truth generally is. Thanks, Dad. Thanks for caring enough to watch. Thanks for recording. Thanks for reminding me that I can learn.

Chapter Twenty

Marbles Now or Horses Later?

Dad chose unique methods of schooling me in finance. He realized my eventual inheritance required tools for proper handling. From age eight on, each week Dad and I had our Monday afternoon date. Each week he gave me a dollar to spend. I could blow it on candy or save up for something meatier. Many Mondays found us at the Brentwood Country Mart cruising both the toy store and the Brentwood saddlery. What a plethora of distractions. We'd fortify ourselves with hot dogs, fries, and lemonade before surveying the territory. The toy store held model horses, model cars, super Pinky balls, Legos, and Barbies of every description. The tack shop sported saddles, bridles, amazing silver belt buckles, boots, romal reins, roller bits, monogrammed horse blankets, chaps, brushes for applying Hoofbrite . . . oh my. One dollar. Saving for a Barbie took months. Romal reins? Forget it. The saddlery took birthdays to conquer. It's Pavlovian, but I still salivate at the thought of Lexol saddle soap. So, the choice was to drool over the big stuff or to go for the instant gratification of marbles or jacks. Must be where my passion for super Pinky balls began. Excellent bouncers. However . . . what could eclipse the feeling of elation at waiting months for a prized plastic cantering Thoroughbred or Malibu Barbie? I'd done it! I'd saved! I'd staved off temptation and here were my rewards. I'd canter laps all around the house with the booty from my conquest.

Dad reasoned it was never too early to learn economics. By age twelve I was well versed in the concept of tax brackets, percentages, and where our money went. I even signed my own quarterly taxes. Still, having a personal income was a matter of pride. My stash! Jobs varied from babysitting to clerking at the Pacific Palisades Village Store and checkout girl at Malibu's Rainbow Grocery. My earnings meant empowerment. I could spend unhindered by parental forces.

For my sixteenth birthday, Dad bought me a brown Honda Civic four door. It was a great car; it never broke down. Not once. A few years later, I hungered for something a little racier, something that would show me off for my junior year at Stanford. The agreement was that if I saved half of the difference between my old and new cars, Dad would cover the remaining half. I waitressed six days a week all summer. Dad and Barbara occasionally visited me at the Pioneer Boulangerie in Santa Monica. Big pressure. With six or seven tables to tend there was no time for chat. Dad loved seeing me hustle. They were excellent tippers and Dad quite liked the rumaki appetizers, so it was all good. Within three months I made a few thousand dollars and a beeline for a convertible VW. The scary part was negotiating for my periwinkle blue beauty. Dad sent me to the dealer with his secretary in tow to witness the bargaining. Dad abdicated his customary position alongside me. He well knew that "CG's" presence at a dealership would immediately drive up the price. It was a several-day process of haggling our way through L.A. Why not just buy it at the closest place? "Make them compete for your business, Jennifer. Watch your back. We know you want the car, but that guy wants a commission. You've always got to think about what's in it for the other guy."

Even in structuring his will Dad chose a thoughtful, educationally sound method of giving. A tiered approach. Dad worried his money might hinder instead of help, like Lotto winners dramatically crumbling under their longed-for blessing. Tendering my transition, the money was placed in a trust, to be doled out in three separate portions at three-year increments. Two trustees were assigned to guide my financial hand. It helped. This was Dad's hard-earned dough. How could I work to respectfully enhance the gift of his money? What if I blew it? What were responsible choices? What did it mean to be a millionaire at twenty-six? Oddly enough, I never once considered not working. Both Mom and Dad's Capricorn work ethic is deeply ingrained. Thank God Dad provided me with the resources to handle my new resources.

My father had a rare combination of traits. He was an artist who perceived himself as a businessman. Dad earned his money and studied to increase it. He loved the stock market. Dad was a blue chip guy, but he followed the latest trends, bulls and bears, even if he wasn't a big risk taker himself. Still, money was never his main focus. Dad wanted me to learn to cut hair. "If there's a war, soldiers always need a good haircut." He was passing on millions, but plan B was still worth considering. The point was learning, being responsible, and appreciating life's gifts. Money was a gift to respect and work with. He wasn't driven to make more more more. He was happy.

Chapter Twenty-One
The Phantom Pot Smoke

Dad could be a bit extreme at times. In tenth grade, I was "caught" with eye shadow. Preparing to mail a longed-for sweater to my boarding school, Dad happened upon the offensive brown and gold multipack among my things. It looked like a mini artist's palette with a brush/wand in the center. Spiffy. It was in my closet, at home—I wasn't even wearing it! Mere possession of the stuff obliterated all allowance for a few months. The sexy adult eye glitter had taken major effort to procure. If only he'd known I'd stolen it from the Colony mart . . . No allowance for a year? There was no possibility of buying the stuff, after all. Steve, the store's owner, might have ratted me out. "Mr. Grant, Jennifer was seen buying eye shadow." NEVER! I loitered in the makeup aisle for weeks after school plotting my crime. The plan: wait until Steve was busy filling a prescription, ensure his distance from the security mirrors by listening for the movement of the rolling pharmaceutical racks, pretend to be looking at the Luden's cough drops, and woosh! grab the stuff off the wall. I wore my blue parka to hide the square bulge in my pocket. Getting that Maybelline was a coup. Twenty years later I saw Steve at the same Super Care Drugs and confessed my crime. What was the interest on that $4.99 item? We shared a good laugh.

Dad was not a fan of artifice, in any form. Fussiness bothered him. I'm not sure where the saying "never gild the lily" originates, but I heard it all the time. Meaning, to work at beauty is a paradox. Working at it means you've missed the point. Makeup was a huge offender in Dad's book. Nature drew a woman's face—how could cosmetics enhance that? Mucking about with makeup was stupidity. "Terrible stuff. It makes you look like a clown, stains your clothes, and tastes awful." Sparingly used, makeup was acceptable, but never preferable. I remember going to visit my father for one of his "Evenings with Cary Grant." Dad visited community colleges, where he sat for question and answer sessions in packed auditoriums. Dad was candid, natural, visibly at ease onstage, and great with the impromptu response. I was in college. My boyfriend Mack and I drove to hear Dad speak and eat dinner with him and Barbara. At the time I was into a golden-hued lipstick. Very frosty. On my return from the ladies' room that evening Dad remarked, "What is that horrid sparkly stuff all over your lips?" Mack laughed. "It's awful. And why are you wearing so much mascara?" It was true. Mimicking an early Madonna phase, I had caked the stuff on. It even felt cumbersome. Dad asked Mack what he thought. "I agree with you, she looks much better without it." A compliment, but I saw it as only an indictment of my taste. Dad enjoyed individuals, not their accoutrements. He admired natural beauties, like Jacqueline Bisset, Diane Keaton, and Grace Kelly. These women didn't cover themselves in "colored goo."

I could live without makeup . . . for the most part, I still do. Then there was the issue of the phantom pot smoke. Once, when I was fifteen or sixteen, I had five or six friends over for a dinner party

Behind the backstretch of Hollywood Park racetrack, circa 1978.
Dad watched for hours as I tended to my first horse, Specks.

at 9966. Happily, Dad left us to ourselves. For an hour or so things went just fine, until Dad called me to his room. "Who is smoking pot?!" Oh dear. He smelled my breath. Phew . . . innocent . . . but what of the rest of the crew? Was it my wild "long-haired" surfer boyfriend? No clue. Tail tucked, I approached the group, but no one copped to it. Was Dad imagining the pot smoke? Had one of my friends snuck out and lit up a joint without telling me? Never. Dad had a pretty good sniffer, but could his sometimes hypervigilant ways have created pot smoke out of . . . a gust of fertilizer? What is certain is that everyone had to leave, pronto. That was it for my wild party career at 9966.

Dad was serious about my curfew. At fifteen it was ten thirty. At sixteen and seventeen it jumped to 11 p.m. Even in college, at twenty years old, eleven thirty was tops. Tardiness wasn't an option. Tardiness meant Dad would worry. I could feel it brewing from miles away. By ten forty-five, I was on edge. Will there be traffic? Will we make it home on time? Dad always waited up. He waited for my "good night" from the hall. When I was fifteen, my friend Jonathon and I exited *Raging Bull* somewhere midway because we'd underestimated the film's running time. If late, I might suffer the silent treatment. Nothing was worse than the silent treatment.

When Dad got mad he shut up. If he were forced to speak, he would do so only in a low, lethargic tone. As if he were communicating with a moron robot. The silent treatment slayed me. I'd been careless. He'd lost sleep. Silence made the whole house gray. Dad used the method with Barbara, too. Whichever one of us wasn't on the silent treatment received extra sweet attention. The good one seemed a perfect peach. This punctuated the evildoer's woe. Three days was max. Three days of the silent treatment was eternity. Generally, a day or two sufficed. By day three all the wind was knocked out of my self-righteous sails. It worked. Suffice it to say I was rarely late.

Growing up, it was all too important for me to please my father. Pleasing him, I errantly thought, meant being perfect. If that's a normal childhood illusion, it was certainly exacerbated by having an iconic dad. Here's the guy I look up to for everything. Oh, and by the way, so does the rest of the world. He's *the* the. So if he thinks I'm messing up, one long internal scream, and then . . . better fix it fast.

Dad's criticisms crushed me, but I bounced back. In sixth grade I approached Dad for help on a creative writing project. Can't remember the topic. I quite liked my handiwork and craved applause. His critique was gentle, specific, and direct. Edit this or that, clean up this or that, and well done. Wait a minute, something needed to be changed? It wasn't the best thing ever? He was right . . . imperfection revealed! Fix it fast! Grants are perfect, right? We just start that way. Who am I? I thought my name was Grant. No pressure. Then again, Dad had certain less than perfect traits. For instance, he was consistently in a terrible humor for the two or three days that preceded travel. He skulked and whined about the house. Some unarticulated fear, perhaps? The silent treatment could be regarded as a fault as well, it was truly extreme at times. Though his silence cut like a knife, lucky for me, another Grant trait is resiliency. Bruise easy, heal fast. I'm still that way. I've generally used Dad's unflinching eye on myself, without always remembering his unflinching love.

LOVE IS THE THOUGHT BEHIND HAPPINESS

Dad was generally a happy man. I believe he was happy because he filled himself with conscious, loving thoughts. I've heard it said that "sometimes love isn't enough." Well, that depends on one's definition of love. My father made a world of love: love of people, love of learning, love of nature, love of country, love of one's fellow man, love of family, love of beauty, love of the arts, love of . . . you get the picture. Dad closed most of his letters with the phrase "happy thoughts." The way I break it down, if thoughts produce actions, then happy thoughts produce kind and loving actions.

GIVE PRICELESSLY

My father earned his wealth and he enjoyed sharing it. Perhaps he earned his wealth *because* he enjoyed sharing it. He rarely, if ever, flaunted his money. Nothing overly extravagant or self-aggrandizing. Dad was sensible with money and he didn't care what others thought of his choices. He made the dough and he wasn't going to waste it by carelessly tossing it about. Giving was never about money. Giving only cost if it wasn't of service. A gift should truly be of benefit to its recipient. Dad gave for the sake of giving, because he enjoyed it.

Dad's choice, Dodgers season tickets, were the perfect light-spirited gift. They were a minor extravagance, but one he didn't

CARY GRANT   2nd June, 1983.

My dear Jennifer.

On this, your Graduation Day at Santa Catalina School, I am
extraordinarly proud of you: of all you have accomplished,
of the manner in which you've always comported yourself, of
your sense of humour and justice, of your intelligence and
of how beautifully you have grown in every way.

Well now, on such occasions, it is customary to give a watch
or, sometimes even, a first car; but you already have those
things.

It has been puzzling me to find a suitable present. So,
although you may not be quite old enough for the gift that
accompanies this letter, I thought you would enjoy having,
keeping, and eventually, wearing it: especially because
you see it belonged to my mother who seldom wore such things
but who would have adored to see you today, just as I do
today and all days, dearest Jennifer.

    With Barbara's and my love always,

                    Dad.

*This letter was accompanied by Grandmother Elsie's circular
diamond brooch. I treasure it still.*

take for granted. Great loge-level seats. When we were unable to attend he could have sold the tickets or offered them to friends, but instead Dad gave them to people who may not otherwise have had the opportunity to go to a game. Tickets probably meant more to the "fellows who worked at the market" than they did to the Sinatras, for instance. Dad would pop into Market Basket on occasion and have a little Dodgers chat with the guys about the previous night's game, who threw what, and what he'd missed. After months of this, we found out they'd been scalping the tickets. Dad was so let down. He couldn't stomach people who easily contrived lies, particularly in the face of generosity. How unkind. Thereafter Dad went to the guards at the Colony gate, and having issued fair warning about not duping him, he found a way to give the tickets to guys who actually enjoyed *going* to the games. I dug Dad's sports talk. Whenever we'd come through the gate . . . "Mr. Grant, did you see Garvey's throw to second?"

Common ground.

Dad wasn't a fan of overly lavish displays, at least not in the worldly sense. Our home was beautiful and not a mansion. What did we need with a mansion? Our parties were small parties. We had a white, modern-looking oval table that at most sat fourteen. You could see and hear everyone. The mood was festive and intimate. Barbara made scrumptious, home-cooked meals and decorated the table with her own arrangements of flowers. Dad was so proud. I understand why. Our home had love, warmth, and personal care. It was overflowing. That's what we shared when we shared meals. Abundant love. One may enjoy huge parties, or elaborately catered affairs, but no event feeds my soul as well as an intimate, homemade dinner. Dad, Barbara, and I were largely homebodies. We ate at home most nights. When we did eat out, if Dad liked the place, and the service, he would act on it. If the staff was attentive, but not overly ingratiating, or if the waiter showed uncommon kindness by, say, asking if we wanted to have the car brought around, Dad might leave a huge tip. Double-the-cost-of-the-meal-sized tip. But only as a surprise, never the rule. He liked rewarding work well done.

Dad urged me never to buy him a gift—"I already have everything I need. Make me something, instead." So . . . I learned to knit. My grandma Clara Friesen taught me. Grandma was a spectacular knitter. She made beautiful throw blankets. My favorite was orange with large black horses on it (Grandma had given me the choice of colors and I was a big horse fan). I was just okay at knitting. Straight lines were my forte. Knit one, pearl two. The turn at the end of the line was a bit challenging. Still, I managed to make Dad a dark blue scarf one Christmas. I thought he could wear it over his suits. Like the cashmere scarves he wore so handsomely. Well, Dad *loved* the scarf. Not because of my knitting acumen. No. Dad treasured it because he found the stitch I had dropped precisely in its center. Oh, it made him smile. He would show it to his friends, sticking his finger through the dropped stitch, "Look! My Jennifer made this."

Dad took care of people. He took care with tiny thoughtful gestures. When I was too young to remember, Dad chose to treat Willie and me to dinner at Madame Wu's.

Auntie Sylvia hadn't yet met Willie, so Dad sent a note in advance to let her know that Willie was a black woman. Certainly Auntie Sylvia would've recognized that fact.

Was Dad's note unnecessary? What if we'd arrived unannounced? My guess is that knowing Sylvia's savvy, Dad wanted to make sure we'd be properly seated. L.A. now is a far better picture in terms of racial equality than the Los Angeles of the early seventies.

Auntie Sylvia knew her patrons. If there were bigots in the house, she could steer us clear of them. Truly. Dad was pretty far out in his caring quota. He cared about everyone's happiness and did his level best to ensure that if you were with him, you were well protected.

Sometimes I imagine Dad's responses to life in 2010. The world has changed in myriad ways since my father left us. We're all closer now. Information at the touch of a button. The global community.

Dad would marvel over the Internet, cloning, stem cells, Google, blogs, but I can just hear the Brit in him riffing on some of it. "Excuse me," he'd say, "I have a very important [pause, then with added emphasis] *blog* to write. Couldn't they come up with a more dignified term? Bloggers?" When Dad moved to Los Angeles, Burbank was still covered in horse trails. Dad used to gape at the 10 freeway overpass on the way to Palm Springs. The engineering boggled his mind. "Imagine"—he'd look up in awe—"someone actually built that." He presaged that in my lifetime there might be shuttles to the moon . . . and that perhaps I would visit. "Oh darling, the many things you'll know that I don't! Isn't it wonderful." Mmm . . . perhaps. Dad was happy because he loved well.

Chapter Twenty-Two

Don't Marry the Guy
You Break the Bed With

I've often wondered if Dad wanted a son. I know Dad wanted me, but perhaps if he were given the choice, he'd have chosen a boy? How different it would have been for him to raise a son. Imagine being that son. The pressure to be charming, wildly talented, suave, stylish, graceful, dapper . . . the all-around guy. Perhaps it was a relief to have a girl. By the time I was born, Dad was in his sixties, and not much into athletics. An occasional swim suited him. That, walking around doing the day-to-days, and breathing in and out was enough. So no need for the whole "teach me soccer and football" at the local park routine.

I enjoyed spectator sports just as much as Dad. At ball games we ate smoky foot-long Dodger Dogs (Dad liked mustard and relish) with chocolate malteds and listened to Vin Scully announce. So, while we didn't pitch and catch fastballs together, we devoured baseball games from the O'Malleys' box. Maybe having a daughter was a simple case of karma. With a daughter Dad might examine his own conscience. How had he treated women as a boy? A young man? A star? Was he fair to women? What inequities from his past might he project onto my suitors? Dad used to say that I was "just his type." I look like my mom, so that makes sense. As far as other characteristics, while I'm not exactly sure to what he was referring, Barbara and I share a love of nature, quiet, home, and kindness, which suited Dad well. Not sure if that served much comfort when the boys came a-callin' for his pip of a daughter.

At a certain point, Dad dutifully unleashed me to the wonderful world of boys. He'd taught me to ride a tricycle and a ten-speed, to swim freestyle and backstroke, to sit a trot, to modulate my voice, to calculate taxes, and to eat marmalade on muffins. His general directive with all things was "Start slow." One thing he couldn't instruct me in (much to his chagrin) was the opposite sex. In Dad's eyes, no

Dad always found a way to get through.

```
uuu   Telegram
western union

913A PDT AUG 8 72 LA090
SSU026 L ILE0512  VIA ITT 1041/08
AWE593 VIA ITT-CTB815 TX847307
USNX CO GBLB 038
LONDONLB TLX 38 8 1525
WEAVER CHEZ GRANT 9966 BEVERLEY GROVE DRIVE
BEVERLEYHILLSCALIFORNIA USA
PLEASE EXPLAIN TO DEAR JENNIFER AND WILLIE ABSOLUTELY
IMPOSSIBLE TO REACH LONDON INTERNATIONAL OPERATORS IN
ORDER TO TELEPHONE THEM STOP HAVE TRIED EVERY DAY
STOP REGARDS AND SEND LOVE
        CARY
COL 9966 BEVERLEY GROVE DRIVE
NNNN
```

SF-1201 (R5-69)

boy was ever good enough for me. At the dating age of sweet sixteen, reluctantly, he let me go. More than any other endeavor, Dad cautioned, "For God's sake, darling, go slowly."

In my experience, most parents tutor their children in love as though breeding livestock: look for lineage, a prominent name, money, marry into a "good family," or some such fascinating characteristics. Dad did nothing of the sort. In fact, Dad often cautioned, "You know, you may have a lot more money and a great deal more advantages than the man you fall in love with. That's all right. If you believe in the man, stand by him. It's tough to make a living." Whoa. Dad was a scrapper who'd made his way up the ladder. He believed in self-determination and he believed in love. He wanted me to have options besides the guys who look good on paper. Pretty revolutionary for a dad, I find.

Dad's only advice on relationships was "Don't marry the guy you break the bed with." Well, that about says it, Dad. Guess he'd been there, done that. Dad's quip on sex, "Every generation thinks they discovered it. Take a look at that filled-to-capacity football stadium. See all those people? Imagine how much sex it took to create them." Clearly attraction was important to Dad, but he "got" that there's more to the picture. After Mom, Dad had only two semiserious girlfriends before he met Barbara. Both women were British. They were friends, mostly. They laughed a good deal and I was usually in on the joke. Otherwise, all women generally doted on Dad the way women dote on Cary Grant. Dad treated men and women very similarly. Perhaps he flirted with no one, or perhaps he flirted with everyone.

Chapter Twenty-Three
Polishing an Academy Award

Treasures throughout my home bespeak his life. His books grace my bookshelves. "From your *Notorious* and *Indiscreet* friend," Ingrid Bergman. "For Cary, One of the best I've ever known, and my pal," Mervyn LeRoy. His Fabergé clock graces my desk: "Cary—for 16 years of devoted service to Fabergé." Dad's Academy Award sits on my mantelpiece. People are drawn to it. How much does it weigh? The award needs a bit of polish at present and I'm miffed about it. Wouldn't want to tarnish an Academy Award. Blasphemous. How does one go about such a thing? Google "How to polish an Academy Award?" These are the strange moments of inheritance. Lest I momentarily forget my lineage, my surroundings remind me.

Dad was an avid reader of nonfiction. After devouring the daily newspapers he fed his mind with books on American and European history and political autobiographies. While sifting through some of the treasures Dad gave me, I lit on Dad's ex libris: "I shall pass through this world but once. Any good therefore that I can do or any kindness that I can show to any human being, let me do it now. Let me not defer or neglect it for I shall not pass this way again."

Chapter Twenty-Four
The Leach Potato Wart Cure

In terms of Dad's pre-me life, here's what little I know. Dad's mom was Elsie and his dad was Elias Leach. My grandparents. He was raised an only child in Bristol, England. His father wasn't around a lot. Dad was a troublemaker at school, and the way he described it, he liked to jump atop the wall to the girls' locker room. In our equivalent to sixth grade, that propensity got him kicked out. Dad then found a more profitable use for his acrobatic skills. He joined the Pender Troupe, with whom he traveled to America. He shared memories of walking on stilts and introducing shows by running onto the stage and diving, headfirst, into small invisible trapdoors in the wooden floor. No wonder he later loved the circus. The only other relatives I knew were Eric and Maggie Leach. Eric was Dad's mother's sister's son, Dad's cousin. Maggie and Eric were the British Frick and Frack. Ever sweet, hospitable souls with lilting voices and little round cherubic features. They were side by side for life. I never met Dad's dad. Sadly my grandpa, handsome Elias, died young. I was too young to really remember meeting my grandmother. I believe I traveled to Bristol just twice to see her, once when I was a wee babe with Mom and Dad, and then again at the age of two or three. Dad rarely if ever spoke of his parents. My memories are some amalgamation of photographs, audiotapes, and distant flashes of my grandmother, but too disparate to assemble into coherent thought.

As most fans know, Dad's original name was Archibald Alexander Leach. For acting purposes he was asked to change it. Dad was given a list of forenames and a list of surnames from which to choose. At that time shorter names were in vogue. I'm quite happy he chose the name Grant. It's a term that connotes giving. Quite the opposite of Leach, thank you very much. Geographically and emotionally, Dad moved a great distance from his parents and his roots. His name accurately reflected the distance traveled.

Dad's previous marriages went undiscussed as well. Nothing taboo; I simply never asked. He was married five times. I knew the names of his first three wives and vaguely knew their faces. That was all fine, and beyond that, it was history. Where had they met? What was the initial attraction? Where were the women from? What were their hobbies? Did they have pet nicknames? Favorite joints around town? Where did they live? What did Dad learn? Why did they divorce? Did he miss any of them? Regrets? No clue. Life in the present occupied us. The past played little role. That was then. He had no meaningful contact with his exes, aside from my mother. So we moved on. There were some sweet reminiscences, but that was about it.

How did Dad spend his childhood? Who were his friends? What was his room like? Did he have a favorite toy? Did he tell me? Have I forgotten? I've only the tiniest glimpses. For instance, Dad tried to cure me of my warts. They were mortifying! One lumpy grossness on the inside of my right palm and one on my left index finger. Tenacious things. Dad told me he knew of an old English trick certain to rid me of the buggers. The process was to rub a potato on the warts and then plant said potato in the garden. Somehow the potato was meant to magnetize the warts to it. Every morning I awakened to see if my warts had made their pilgrimage home. Damn. No luck. Thereafter Compound W was applied daily. They grew back and back and back again. Finally, after years, I shaved them off. Dad claimed I didn't have enough faith in the potato. Apparently it had worked for him as a child. Who taught him that trick? My grandma Elsie Leach? Did he plant the potato in his garden? Did they have a garden?

For all too brief an interval, Dad had a stepson named Lance. Lance's mother, Barbara Hutton, was Dad's second wife. In the day-to-days of their living together, if the telephone rang while Dad was in a meeting, six- or seven-year-old Lance greeted the caller with "I'm sorry, Mr. Grant can't come to the phone now. . . . He's in confidence." Dad thought it a superior term to "conference." He found the error so spot-on charming that he refused to correct Lance. Some eager caller eventually let on, much to Dad's chagrin. That was the sole story Dad recounted of Lance. That and Lance's death. Lance was a pilot who died in a crash at the age of thirty-six. Whenever Dad spoke of Lance his eyes softened and his gaze thoughtfully sloped. These are the things he told me. That's all I know for sure.

Occasionally stories of Dad's pre-Jennifer life find their way to me. At a recent dinner party I was introduced to Nena Woolworth, a cousin of Barbara Hutton's. She pulled me aside to relate how very special my father was to her family. "He was the only one who really loved her (Barbara Hutton) for who she was. He was the only one who never went after her estate . . . he was the one bright spot." How sweet of her to share this with me. Dad's love had integrity. He could never demean himself and their relationship by going after his previous wife's wealth.

In Dad's later years he didn't sleep much. He woke most nights at two or three a.m., and, unable to return to sleep, he would read for an hour or two. Sometimes he barely slept. He was a middle-of-the-

These are the moments I remember best: the way, childlike, his face lit up and his feet danced about at the sight of this homemade cake. January 18, 1982.

night worrier. He stressed about doing the right thing in life. Dad bore a rigid conscience. One cross word or careless remark deeply troubled him. Was this tendency for worry rooted in his childhood? As a child I didn't have much curiosity about his history. Context may not have occurred to me. Dad related some quaintly amusing anecdotes, the "I remember whens" that get repeated year after year. I gathered it wasn't easy. At Christmastime, prior to opening our truckloads of gifts, he'd say, "You know, when I was a boy, in wartime England, we were lucky if we got an orange in our stocking. . . . That was it. An orange was a true delight."

Why don't I research more about Dad's past? Aren't I interested? Yes and no. In our heart of hearts, I believe we all know the

"Jennifer's first drawing, Aug. 16, 1967. Beverly Hills. 620 Foothill Road." In his exuberant way, Dad labeled some of my chicken-scratch drawings "mini Picassos."

LIKE GROUCHO MARX I AM ADAMANT ABOUT NOT WANTING EITHER FLOWERS OR EULOGIES

WHEN I'M GONE, UNLESS THE EULOGY WOULD IMPRESS MY DAUGHTER *and my dear wife* THAT I DID THE BEST

I KNEW HOW IN EVERY PHASE OF LIFE. FOR MYSELF AND OTHERS AROUND ME. WHEN I

DIE, I JUST WANT TO DIE. AND BE REMEMBERED MOSTLY AS A GOOD SON TO MY MOTHER

AND FATHER, AND A GOOD FATHER BY MY DAUGHTER: *and a good husband to my wife*.

KING LEAR:"HOW SHARPER THAN A SERPENTS TOOTH IS AN UNGRATEFUL CHILD!" STILL
ONE FATHER WHOSE VERY NAME CALLS UP VISIONS OF LUXURY. YET HIS CHILDREN--AND,
LATER, HIS GRANDCHILDREN--WERE GIVEN ALLOWANCES OF 25 CENTS A WEEK AND REQUIRED TO
SAVE 10% AND GIVE 10% TO CHARITY! THIS PATRIARCHS NAME WAS JOHN D ROCKEFELLER

HAPPINESS IS BROUGHT ABOUT BY SELF RESPECT, SERVICE TO OTHERS, AND WORK WELL-DONE.
IT'S A STATE OF MIND AND NO AMOUNT OF MONEY CAN ASSURE US OF IT. WE CANNOT GIVE
IT TO OUR CHILDREN. THEY MUST EARN IT. SO MANY CHILDREN OF WEALTHY PARENTS HAVE
ANTICIPATED THEIR PARENTS DEATH SO THEY CAN INHERIT THEIR FORTUNE, BUT THERE ARE
SO MANY BETTER THINGS THAT THEY CAN BE BEQUEATHED. HONESTY AND INTEGRITY ARE
ABOVE STOCKS AND BONDS AND THE PRIDE OF A LIFE LIVED UNSELFISHLY.

LARRY OLIVIER ON OCCASION NOEL COWARDS DEATH: "ANY COMPREHENSIVE APPRECIA=
TION OF HIS LIFE AND TIMES AND WORK IS A PRODIGIOUS TASK FOR ONLY THE MOST
PAINSTAKING OF RESEARCHERS, AND THE MOMENT FINDS ME BEREFT OF ANY OTHER
EXPRESSION EXCEPT THAT OF GRIEF."

A PLACE WHERE THE STRONG ARE JUST AND THE WEAK SECURE

TAKE TIME FOR 10 THINGS

1. TAKE TIME TO WORK: IT IS THE PRICE OF SUCCESS.
2. TAKE TIME TO THINK: IT IS THE SOURCE OF POWER.
3. TAKE TIME TO PLAY: IT IS THE SECRET OF YOUTH.
4. TAKE TIME TO READ: IT IS THE FOUNDATION OF KNOWLEDGE.
5. TAKE TIME TO WORSHIP: IT IS THE HIGHWAY OF REVERENCE AND CLEARS THE
   DUST OF EARTH FROM OUR MINDS.
6. TAKE TIME TO HELP: IT IS THE SOURCE OF TRUE HAPPINESS.
7. TAKE TIME TO LOVE: IT IS A SACRAMENT OF LIFE.
8. TAKE TIME TO DREAM: IT HITCHES THE SOUL TO THE STARS.
9. TAKE TIME TO LAUGH: IT IS THE SINGING THAT HELPS WITH LIFE'S LOADS.
10. TAKE TIME PLAN: IT IS THE SECRET OF BEING ABLE TO OBTAIN SECURITY,
    MONEY AND TIME IN ORDER TO ENJOY THE FIRST NINE TO THE FULLEST.

"WHAT KIND OF CHRISTMAS STORY DO YOU WRITE WHEN YOU'RE NOT SURE HOW MUCH
STRING IS LEFT IN YOUR BALL OF STRING?". BUGS BARE ON HIS LAST CHIRSTMAS IN
HOSPITAL FOLLOWED BY "OH TO BE SEVENTY AGAIN WITH THE WIND AND RAIN IN MY
HAIR"

*In case he left something out, Dad saved for me these musings on living,
dying, and the art of happiness. Later, in his own print,
he added Barbara's name to the typed page.*

skinny on people and situations. We unconsciously block what's too much for us to process. So, somewhere inside . . . it's all there. Other than that, I prefer knowing what I know. I remember his saying this and that, wearing these shoes, and eating this type of ham, and before speeches how he would always . . . type of remembrance. It feels safer to me. While I might discover the links to myriad minuscule and not so minuscule pieces of the puzzle by digging into Dad's lineage and pre-Jennifer choices, the likelihood is as good that I'd burrow myself a mudhole. Information arises when and if it needs to. That's enough for me. I'll stick with my trusty experience as a guide.

While there's a lot of stuff I certainly don't know, there's also a lot I do. For instance, Dad had a very unique yawn. He didn't just plain old "I'm tired" yawn. Dad's yawns were multisyllabic and he made the most of every one. Dad's yawn had flourish. The sound was something like "aaaaa yeeee haaaaw haaaaaw." It had volume. It was an announcement. The big bear part of Dad, standing tall, head back, arms outstretched to the world, announced that his day was complete. It was time for rest. His yawns were celebratory. As if to say, "Another day well done." How many people know about my father's round tuits? On outings, he often carried a convenient little gag along. A round tuit is an inch-wide wooden disc with the word "TUIT" emblazoned across its center. Around to it. A round tuit. When greeting friends, he'd ask, "Did you get around to it?" Brows furrowed in response—what had they forgotten? They'd promised Cary Grant something marvelous and they'd slipped. "Uh, around to what?" Now they were hooked; Dad loved it. Next he'd feign concern to really pull them in. "Oh, come on now . . . tell me. . . . Did you get around to it?" "Oh, Cary . . . I don't know what you mean." "Well then"—he'd hand them the disc—"You can relax. Now you have." Goofball. This stuff lives in me. The many oddities, the many glances, the many sighs, snores, hugs, pauses, prat falls, and more . . . that's just plenty for me.

Chapter Twenty-Five
My Father Was a Hottie

As one might well imagine, the ladies constantly swooned over Dad. Truly, women of all ages gazed, half-stoned-looking, as though they'd tripped into Jesus incarnate complete with circumfluent halo. They'd even cozy up to me to pose for Dad. I could feel it. Their peripheral focus was on me, but the real focus was on Dad. Like those Southern belles who so eyelash-battingly lob one comment whose subterranean drift runs, "Aren't I the ideal stepmother? Don't I look good? I'm sexy, I'm sweet, I love your daughter. . . ." Run, Dad!

Everywhere I turn it seems my father's looks are being held up as the definition of handsome. Given, he was gorgeous, but clearly there's more to it. I can certainly think of some male supermodels who are all that . . . but no bag of chips. If it's true that girls just wanna have fun, then perhaps that was icing on Dad's attractiveness. He made life fun. It's absurd to presume it was all about the outer picture. Even the bankable on his own merits talent of George Clooney recently did a seemingly conscious imitation of Dad in a *Vanity Fair* photo shoot. Dad in present tense. Was he spoofing my father? Perhaps playing into the joke of "it's all about looks." I'm happy that he's representing Dad as an environmentally conscious, talented, beautiful man. Clooney waited until this phase of his life to don my father's style. Post *Syriana.* Post becoming a producer and director. Elegant.

My favorite of Dad's physical characteristics were his hands. Beautiful, powerful, large, masculine, broad palmed, long fingered, vascular, could-do-the-work hands that held elegance in their assured gentility. He had nice feet, too, but his hands were the pièce de résistance.

As far as attire goes, my father is still known for his classic, timeless taste. True style. He's the all-time best-dressed lists go-to guy. Books are sold on his sense of style alone. Every time I flip open a magazine there he is, looking stunning in a suit. *GQ* recently touted his signature large, black, square eyeglasses as the new in thing. New indeed. I only wish I had his fashion sense.

Dad's style had a system behind it. Dad signaled approval with "My how smart you look." Interesting. How "smart." Not how sexy or pretty or stunning. How smart. It implies the look has good, practical thought. One is appealing to the eye because the choice is about more than egotistical whim. It's, let's say, environmentally correct. Dad and I shopped at the Gap together. Dad loved the Gap. It spoke to his uniform theory and the store was decently priced. Dad thought schoolchildren wearing uniforms eliminated competition and helped even the playing field. At the time, the Gap was stocked with one basic type of jean. Dad wore Levi's 501s. I don't recall him ever purchasing new blue jeans on our outings. Blue jeans were built to last and got better with age. Also, they weren't covered in logos. Dad hated logos. "If they're going to plaster their name all over me, they should pay me to advertise their product." Dad was somewhat prescient, because today's gang violence is often tipped by designer shoes and clothing. Yes, the roots run far deeper, but the surface picture is kids killing kids over shoes. So I guess Dad's uniform theory holds water. He did allow a single exception. When Polo shirts were first on the scene, I requested one. Luckily for me, Dad okayed the mini Polo logo and Beverly Hills is a small town. Dad ran into Ralph Lauren and forwarded my request. Ralph delivered big. Dad doled out my goodies on a weekly basis . . . summer shades, autumn shades, I had about fifteen Polo shirts. Thank you, Ralph.

On a recent shopping/browsing escapade I happened upon boots that were fashioned to look old. The toes were faded, the heels were scratched, and the rubber soles were worn on the corners. The conceptual design? Let's make boots for people who have so many shoes that they've no time to wear them? Dad's voice boomed through my brain. "What a scam! Imagine that, paying for worn boots. Pay me to wear those and then they can sell them to someone else." He'd likely feel the same way about prefaded denim, another manufacturer's ruse.

Around the house, Dad was completely casual. Of course, even his casual had flair. When I was a child, in the mornings and on weekend afternoons, Dad wore beautiful monogrammed pajamas and silk robes. After Barbara moved in, Dad replaced his pj's with caftans. The magical Barbara sewed them for Dad in a rainbow of colors. He practically lived in his linen and cotton Mediterranean tunics. "Great ventilation!"

FORM WITH FUNCTION

If he were to show up today, at my door, he would be in perfect fashion. Dad didn't have one signature outfit, but he stuck to a few favored ensembles. Generally slacks and sweaters, jeans and cotton shirts, or suits and ties. I see him in my favorite of his casual looks: jeans, a worn and therefore faded red shirt with Western-style pockets, a camel-colored cashmere sweater, his silver and turquoise belt buckle, and round-toed cowboy boots. Never the pointed ones. Dad found them silly. "What's the idea behind them?" he'd say. "Unless you need to crush a cockroach in the corner." Even for the purposes of Western-style horseback riding, Dad wore the round-toed boots. Many, if not most, of the "real" cowboys I've met wear round-toed boots, so I suppose there's something to it.

Dad was never a fan of fads. In fact, he deplored them. I remember when men started wearing suits and T-shirts together.

If he happened to see a young "hip" fellow at, let's say, the Directors' Lounge of the racetrack, wearing a dark suit with a T-shirt, he'd scoff, "Doesn't that man know that he's ruining his suit? Ridiculous." Trends were wasteful and impermanent, and in Dad's view trends had been calculated by the fashion industry to keep us at their mercy. If one followed fads, he convincingly argued, one always had to buy the newest latest thing and throw out last week's wares. Dad particularly disliked potentially harmful fads. Bell-bottomed trousers caused bike wrecks. High-heeled wedge shoes made women break their necks. He was dramatic about it, but he was, in essence, correct. He did, however, indulge me by wearing what was in his mind semi-risqué . . . his light pink cotton button-down shirt. Lovely.

Dad's friend Howard Hughes had some of his own ideas about good form. 9966 was a favorite with Howard. I was under the errant impression that he owned it at some point. Wrong. Howard often visited Dad at 9966, dining on steaks and ice cream. Howard bought the property directly above ours, which was a larger lot, and tried to "switch" it with Dad. No dice. So, prior to my birth, if Dad was away on location, Howard often stayed at 9966. When packing to go away on vacation, if I showed up with too much luggage Dad would look at my cases, furrow his brow, and remind me of what he proclaimed to be a Howard Hughes principle: "Did you know that Howard traveled with two suits? Just two. While he was wearing one, the other would be cleaned. Shirts made of a disposable cloth, easily folded and compact. Nothing unnecessary." I'm not exactly sure how I was to apply the principle. Two dresses? Couldn't do it. But then, my dapper father himself didn't apply the rule. One medium-size suitcase was more his style. His cajoling made me a fairly efficient packer, but I'm still dazzled by those women who can pull off a small roll-on case for a week's journey abroad. Good form indeed.

Chapter Twenty-Six
Deeper Waters

1966 · BRISTOL, ENGLAND

Dinner at Eric and Maggie Leach's home.
Mom, Dad, Grandma Elsie, Aunt Maggie, and Uncle Eric.

Family urges Elsie to sing one of her songs. She very sweetly does.

Grandma Elsie: "You taught me how to love you, now teach me
    to forget . . ."

1967 · NEW YORK

Baby Jennifer listens as Daddy slowly demonstrates.

CG: Mouth . . . eyes . . . ears . . . hand . . . Daddy's hands . . .
    together . . . apart.

At twenty I embarked on a semester at sea. I ditched two quarters of Stanford to travel around the world on a cruise ship full of adolescent and elderly adventurers. The itinerary was Spain, Turkey, Greece, Egypt, Israel, Sri Lanka, Taiwan, China, and Hong Kong. Not bad. I sent Dad postcards and mini audiotapes from every port. Israel's Wailing Wall shook me. At eighty-two, Dad was in perfectly good health, but something in me knew him better than surface indicators. It hit me that Dad would die soon. He would leave me, the way his mother left him, the way we all must leave one day. One of those subterranean knowings that you somehow wish could pass by on the breeze, but it nails you, instead. I knew it wasn't imminent, but it was coming. Overcome, my warning system beeped. Grief's tide swelled in me.

Shortly thereafter Dad and I had one of our rare fights. Well, Dad was upset with me. I was ashamed. It felt like a fight. The ship docked in Hong Kong, where I was apprised of the magnificent tailors and their quick custom work. Damn! No more spending money. How to buy Dad a hand-tailored coat? Naturally, ask Dad for more money. No way. Dad was mad. Hong Kong was the last port. I hadn't budgeted properly. No one mentioned the wonderful coats in the itinerary. I'd shot my figurative wad. No time for generosity. When Dad was displeased with me, my head filled with the white noise of shame. If home port sent an unhappy signal, I was rocked to the core. Like Dad, cross words slay me. With Dad on the other side of the globe, at 9966, I could still feel the silent treatment and carried it with me. I walked around glorious Hong Kong feeling shallow, silly, alone. The tone of our argument was unnecessarily and uncharacteristically dark. We were like overexhausted five-year-olds at bedtime. "Stay awake" . . . "I'm not tired, I'm not tired, I don't need to go to bed." If this is possible, I think we were communicating some of our grief beforehand. Somehow we both knew he'd have to go soon, and we were angry about it. I wanted him to stay. He wanted to stay. If I bought him a coat, maybe he'd have to stay and wear it. I was his daughter, he wanted to please me. He'd know not to die. The coat would demand time to be worn.

Mom gave me the money. A gray cashmere coat. I thought the shoulders were a little too round. All he really cared about was the inscription on the inside pocket. "I love you, Dad." Thanks for bailing me out, Mom.

FREEDOM HAS A BEAUTIFUL STRUCTURE

The last time I saw Dad was at home, at 9966. Thanksgiving break for me. I was a student at Stanford at the time, and because it was just before finals and I was worried about my course load, I almost stayed at school over the holiday. Thankfully, my mother talked me into coming home. She reassured me that I'd do fine, I always had. She said that family time and a little break was what I needed. Thank God for a mother's intuition. Thank God I listened.

My boyfriend through most of college, Andy Beyer, came home to Los Angeles with me. We planned to stay at Dad's house for a few days before going to Mom's. Oddly enough, Mom was married to a man who lived literally right around the corner from Dad, so logistics were easy. The night of November 27, 1986, Dad, Barbara, Andy, and I had a quiet supper in the dining room and then retired to my room for a game of Trivial Pursuit. Dad was miraculous with the infuriating game. He'd always complain that he'd forgotten too many important things to be a contender and then pull virtually every answer out of his hat. Typically, I'd pose a question, Dad would look stymied, my teammate and I would grow excited that we'd finally stumped him, and then, out of nowhere, he'd shoot out the answer. Dad's disclaimer: "It's all stored up there somewhere, I guess." So, while we put up a decent enough fight, Dad and Barbara were the easy victors.

Post game time, Dad and Barbara went to bed in their room, Andy took my bedroom, and I went to sleep in the guest room. The guest room was actually my childhood bedroom. It was closer to the master suite and therefore closer to Dad. When I was thirteen we redid the house and my new room was placed at the other end of the hall. That way as a teenager I had a little more space, as did Dad and Barbara, and I could play my music without bugging Dad. That night, I was back in my old room, no music, closer to Dad and Barbara. When I drifted off to sleep, I had the most powerful dream of my life. That night Dad had been as chipper, vital, sharp, and charming as ever, but some other knowing cued my unconscious to the troubles ahead.

In the dream, Barbara, Dad, and I were on a cruise. Dad and I were involved in a painting class. We were painting clowns on velvet. A young, lean, bearded man approached me and bid me ask my father to return to his cabin. I complied. When I got to Dad's room, that same bearded man was with Dad. The man had his hands on my father's shoulders, and my father was kneeling. I was instantly afraid. Dad said I mustn't worry, beckoned me in from the door, and told me that everything was going to be fine. The man never took his hands off of Dad's shoulders. Dad arched his head over and began to vomit blood. Instantly, I awakened from the dream and sat straight up in bed. Something in me knew that he was dying. I quietly ran down to Andy's room and awakened him. Sobbing, I recounted the dream to him.

The young man in the dream had a countenance much like Jesus', and a sweetness that I imagine of him. My mother's side of the family is deeply religious. My father was agnostic. Still, though my father claimed he didn't believe in God, or an afterlife, some actions belied his credo. He generally wore the gifts of a St. Christopher charm and a star of David on a necklace, alongside a charm made from my real, Lucite-encased baby tooth. Dad was neither Jewish nor Christian, but he appreciated the presents as symbols of hope and faith. Another friend gave him the spiritual booklet, "The Daily Word," and thereafter he kept a subscription. He often read me the daily passages. Kind words. Also, he and my mother sent me to a couple of Catholic schools, most notably an all-girl Catholic boarding school. We had mandatory chapel singing and mass each week. One could argue it was for the education, or the strictness of the school's tenets, but I don't think Dad minded the spiritual messages being sent. My father wasn't one to just go along with what he didn't approve of, and he never sanctioned anything as important as my schooling without deep thought. So, while my parents never enforced any prescribed religion, they appreciated the beneficial role spirituality could play for me. Dad seemed to admire the good in all religions without subscribing to one. I've always been spiritually curious. Until the dream, though, I never realized the level of connected feeling I had with Jesus. In the dream, Jesus was the one conducting my father out of this life, and Dad was at peace. It was beautiful.

Remarkably, my father's death, two nights later, bore a startling resemblance to my dream. Dad and Barbara had flown to Davenport, Iowa, where he was to do an "Evening with Cary Grant." Barbara was by his side, and when I asked, she told me the details. The prescient dream helped me. Perhaps we are all infinite, soulful seers, digesting things the way we must to lure us to the next level of understanding.

The morning after the dream, following breakfast together, I gave Dad a huge hug at the back door and said good-bye. I still remember that hug. His hugs were the type that made me feel safe and loved. He had a deep warmth and he fully enveloped me in it. Lovely big bear of a dad. He waved good-bye from the back door, until our car was out of sight.

THE BEASTLY ROAR

On the night of his death, Mom; her husband, Stan; my boyfriend, Andy, and I were all out to dinner. Dad was in Davenport, Iowa. On the way back from dinner, someone called Mom's husband. Stan notified me that I was to call Stanley Fox as soon as we returned to the house. Something in me must have known then. Stanley had never called me before. Why would I need to call Stanley? I said nothing. As soon as we got home I went into the den, alone, and dialed Stanley. I don't remember the words Stanley used . . . all I remember was the otherworldly roar of a cry that erupted from my core. My mother ran into the room. "Thank God she let it out."

Mom and Stan warmed some brandy with honey to help me sleep. They pushed the couches in the living room together so that Andy and I could rest side by side. I slept. Andy watched over me. I remember awakening to his sweet face perched above me. The next morning, bright and early, my dear friend Jonathon Komack appeared to hug me. The men in my life were still there, as Dad would have appreciated, to show me that men could be counted on.

The days after his death were . . . what? Light seemed nonsensical. Words were muted. It was as if I'd slipped into a walking, talking coma. I do remember people coming to the house, but I couldn't tell you who they were. The man who was always there to tell me it was a glorious morning was gone. Could it ever be a glorious morning without him? The one person I remember seeing was Aunt Marje. She brought a truckload of provisions. My body was there, but my spirit was beneath the sea. Somewhere only God knew. Dear Barbara couldn't eat. She lost seemingly half her weight. When others became concerned she'd sit and nibble a bite or two, just to appease.

Dad's death was the biggest shock of my life, one that forever altered my world. As anyone who loses a parent he or she loves knows, my heart was catapulted into new dimensions of sadness, compassion, longing, pain, and bewilderment. It was the end of college for me and the beginning of the real world. Harsh coincidence. The "real world" without Dad. What could that possibly mean? On 9/11, living in downtown Manhattan, I experienced a similar level of shock and heart-opening grief. I'm not comparing the two events themselves—only their earth-shattering effect on me. 9/11 was war in my backyard. As Americans we are blessedly isolated from the brutality that much of the world lives in. As Dad's child, his love shielded me. Dad's death was war on my heart the way 9/11 brought war to my doorstep.

THE HAWK

Nearly six years after Dad died I was married on the front lawn at 9966 Beverly Grove. My then husband and I had a marvelous photographer by the name of Beth Herzhaft. In the midst of our postceremonial family photos, without saying a word, I drifted off from the group. I was attracted by a hawk, and had gently followed it away from my new family. Prior to the ceremony, my father's close friend Quincy Jones had pulled me aside to alert me to the beautiful creature, who was circling the front of the house, just above our heads. Quincy glanced up at the bird and sweetly said, "You see that, he's here . . . with you." Of course, Quincy meant Dad. In Beth's picture I am standing alone, looking up, a bright shaft of light illuminating the air in front of me. There are certain things that are perfectly inexplicable. Sort of wonderfully baffling. Whether you attribute them to God, miracles, "the light," coincidence, science, chemistry, or . . . chocolate, matters not. If you're awake and you notice things, we are constantly surrounded by the sublime. Maybe we all do return home. Or maybe it's just nice to see it that way.

Chapter Twenty-Seven
Live with Death

Parts of me are still in denial. November 29, 2007. Twenty-one years after Dad's death. Earlier in November, my brilliant, effervescent, ninety-nine-year-old grandpa died. I recognized that it was quite near the date of Dad's death, but for the life of me I couldn't have told you the date Dad died. I remember the phone number at 9966 when I was twelve. I remember his birthday. I remember my dog's birthday. But, oh damn it, that day has a way of sneaking up on me. The night of November 28, 2007, I was sad and couldn't figure out why. Just quietly sad. The morning of his death's anniversary an e-mail alerted me to the fact. So that's it. A few more tears . . . a few more tears . . . still. What's the principle at work here? Perhaps we must remember loved ones' deaths with the same gentle grace with which we remember their lives?

On my trips through the letters, one everyday "I love you" note sent to Dad in October 1986 pulled at me. So close to his passing. A letter I'd written blissfully unaware of his imminent departure. My heart cried out. . . . Did I say what I needed to say? Did he know how much I loved him? Would he have stayed longer if I'd called more? What did I miss? If you can hear me, Dad, I'm sorry! If I could've done something, many things, anything . . . if there's anything you want me to do now . . . and I swear to you, I can hear him say, "Be happy, darling."

What would life have been like if Dad had lived longer? Pointless question? Is there a parallel universe? A sliding door picture of the world—is that version of me communicating with this one? Sometimes I still dream of Dad. Most often it's when things are weighing on me, and I need his guidance. Maybe he really visits. Heartwarming to think so. What would he think of this damn war we're in? Dad was a Republican. What would he say about our environment? What would he think of his single daughter choosing to mother a child? Dad was a very open-minded man. A Republican with an open mind. My internalized dad says, "Are you happy? You seem to be happy. You're not hurting anyone, so, okay."

FEBRUARY 28, 1968 · 9966 BEVERLY GROVE DRIVE

Dad and Jennifer drawing babies.

CG: Are you going to have lots of babies when you grow up? Oh
I do hope so.

Dad cooed over my pageboy haircut: "Oh darling, that's your best look. It suits you magnificently. If I were you I would always have one." On the steps leading to the lawn at 9966.

JG: I say.
CG: "I say." That sounds like me, I say.

In the continuing odyssey of my dreams, just before learning of my pregnancy, I had another delightful vision. I dreamed I was hovering over Benjamin Friesen, my mother's recently departed father, my recently departed grandfather. In life, Grandpa Ben was everyone's favorite family member. He had energy enough for five men and a sunny, generous warmth mixed with integrity and candor. He passed away just weeks shy of his one hundredth birthday. Grandpa Ben was reminiscent of Dad. Mom liked to say that she married someone older than her own father, which, oddly enough, made my grandfather younger than my father. In the dream, Grandpa Ben's body rose, and as he turned toward me he "became" my father. Only, in the inimitable language of dreams, Dad didn't exactly look like Dad. His eyes were filled with star light, and, gazing intently at me, Dad was communicating *something*. What was he saying? Two radi-

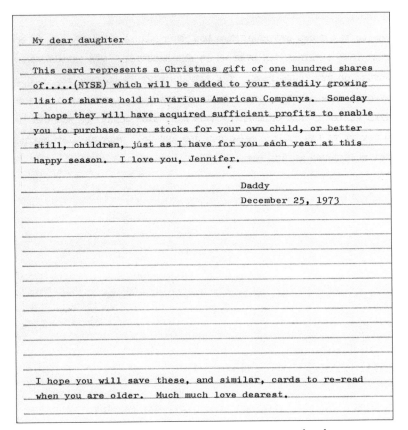

My dear daughter

This card represents a Christmas gift of one hundred shares
of.....(NYSE) which will be added to your steadily growing
list of shares held in various American Companys. Someday
I hope they will have acquired sufficient profits to enable
you to purchase more stocks for your own child, or better
still, children, just as I have for you each year at this
happy season. I love you, Jennifer.

Daddy
December 25, 1973

I hope you will save these, and similar, cards to re-read
when you are older. Much much love dearest.

Dad's sensible, kind tutoring in economics started early.
I was seven when he wrote this card.

ant stars shone out at me. What did it mean? The next night I
dreamed of a single cell, surrounded by the black sky of space, moving about in its gel-like way, with the same two stars inside it. It was
moving, growing, and shifting. What did it mean? Two days after
that second dream I discovered I was pregnant. The stars in the cell
were growing inside me. Was this my signal from the dad in me that
it's all alright? My future baby is part of the same ether, part of the
same magical structure that made my grandfather and my father and

the stars and you and me and everything? Perhaps there's a piece of him in all this, too.

DOUBLE LIVING

Gramercy Park, a private oasis in the middle of Manhattan. A safe haven where you can sit and read a book surrounded by art and lovingly tended gardens. It reminds me of Dad.

Kirk, Barbara, and I scattered his ashes over the sea, near where I used to live in Santa Monica. Is that why I chose the particular residence? To remain near him? His ashes are mixed in all, but he'd forged such a singular form. His dark skin, the smell of that tanned skin, his aching, heart-bursting smile, his sideways half-vaudevillian toe-heel dance into the cupboard with a mimed "ouch" dances, his pink shirts, his beautiful hands, his engulfing hugs, his long spindly legs . . . his being may never be repeated, but life's grace and my dreams remind me.

Perhaps there's also a responsibility that comes with the loss. As Dad's *On Man and Nature* tells us, "On the death of a friend, we should consider that the fates through confidence have devolved on us the task of a double living, that we have henceforth to fulfill the promise of our friends' life also, in our own, to the world."

What must we do to fulfill Dad's promise? What place in us did he awaken and how may we share that place? What stone was left unturned? The consciousness of fulfilling that promise is one way to live with death.

Until one night a few years ago Dad's gray cashmere coat sat in my closet. My dog, Ollie, and I were on our nightly beach stroll when we passed a homeless man curled up near a wall, shielding himself from the cold. Immediate flash to my blanketed beds and fridge full of food. Then the coat. Dad would have wanted me to give it away. Better off warming a live body than sitting in my closet or sold at some auction. Perhaps it kept the man warm. Perhaps there was a better choice?

I do miss the beautiful coat.

Daddy and Jennifer solve word puzzles and riddles out of Wee Wisdom *magazine.*

CG: I'll read a little poem to you and you guess what it is . . .

> *It makes a picture in your mind*
> *Tells where to seek things hard to find*
> *It makes one sad, or mad or glad*
> *It tells of people good or bad*
> *It pleases on a rainy day*

Dad in one of his signature camel-colored cashmere sweaters. I love how gently he regarded my seriousness at Malibu's "shrimp show" horse show. Circa 1978 or 1979.

JG: Oh! Santa Claus!
CG: No, "It." Santa would be "he."

> *It interests when bored with play.*
> *It teaches, informs, entertains*
> *Holds everything from work to games*
> *It transports to exotic places*
> *Tells of all the earth's strange races*
> *It guides, encourages, fills with hope*
> *And helps man realize his scope*

JG [interjecting]: It's God! [At same time] . . . CG: What is it?
CG [laughing with delight]: Oh that's a wonderful answer but that's not the answer I have here. Oh . . . it should be. . . . What do you think the answer is? It makes a picture in the mind.
JG: Heaven?
CG: No, darling. But it's a wonderful guess. Well, the answer is a book. But that was very good. I liked your answer better, I think. . . .

1966 · BRISTOL, ENGLAND

Mom, Dad, and infant Jennifer visit Grandma Elsie in her nursing home.

Grandma Elsie: Archie, you know she's like you. [Jennifer coos] . . . Look at her smiling.
Dad: Good stuff, isn't it?
Grandma Elsie: 'Ello, darling. She's watching Archie to see what he's doing.
Mom: Hello, sweet girl. Jennifer, give a smile, darling.
Dad: Everybody smile.

Acknowledgments

Thank you to the friends whose love, wisdom, and infinite patience inspired me to write this book: Yehuda Berg, Winston Carney, Traylor Howard, Barbara Jaynes, David Jaynes, Quincy Jones, Jonathon Komack, Demi Moore, Ashton Kutcher, Camilla Olsson, Emily Procter, Shalom Sharabi, Barbara Sinatra, Dan Strone, Mark Teitelbaum, Susan Traylor, Victoria Wilson, and Madame Sylvia Wu.

A NOTE ON THE TYPE

The text of this book was set in Garamond No. 3. It is not a true copy of any of the designs of Claude Garamond (ca. 1480–1561), but an adaptation of his types, which set the European standard for two centuries. This particular version is based on an adaptation by Morris Fuller Benton.

COMPOSED BY
*North Market Street Graphics,
Lancaster, Pennsylvania*

PRINTED AND BOUND BY
*Berryville Graphics,
Berryville, Virginia*

DESIGNED BY
Iris Weinstein